Points of
Cosmic Energy

Points of Cosmic Energy

Blanche Merz

Translated from the French by
Michèle Carter Burdet

SAFFRON WALDEN
THE C. W. DANIEL COMPANY LIMITED

First published in French by Georg & Cie, S.A.,
Geneva, Switzerland, and published in Great Britain by
The C. W. Daniel Company Limited,
1 Church Path, Saffron Walden,
Essex CB10 1JP, England

© 1983, 1985 by
Librairie de l'Université, Georg & Cie, S.A.
© 1987 English Translation Michèle Carter Burdet

ISBN 0 85207 194 9

Reprinted 1995

Design and production in association with
Book Production Consultants Plc, Cambridge
Typeset by Cambridge Photosetting Services
Printed and bound in Great Britain by
St Edmundsbury Press Limited, Bury St Edmunds, Suffolk

Contents

Better to light a tiny lamp than to become angry at the darkness.

Chinese proverb

CHAPTER I

Setting the Scene

1. Peering through a Half-Open Door

Our culture has a tendency to transform into rigid dogma any phenomena which it cannot explain, yet in the dim past our ancestors had already created networks of systematic knowledge, systems which today we dare to call outdated.

For such reasons we are going to examine the earth's crust, a crust which reveals grudgingly its capacity to have direct and rapid influence on our daily lives.

A new science has been born without making much noise, without seeking to unleash superficial emotions and curiosities. This science is geobiology, which concentrates on the behaviour and the health of the human being in relation to the precise spot where he lives.

Being sensitive to reality means knowing how to live in harmony with the universe, the earth, the animals, as well as becoming more conscious of one's own personal environment.

One path of our research leads us to certain power points on our globe, places where the field of vibratory intensity has remained intact over the centuries, even the millennia, and has retained a powerful impact over individuals in our time. Our method will be to verify the intentions of the ancient builders when they chose a specific location, a power point, for the construction of a sacred edifice. At the same time we want to take account of those vibrations, those affinities, and those sensitivities which permit us to throw a tangible bridge between the man-antenna of yesteryear and the sophisticated electronic antenna of today. Through the techniques of geobiology we discover that the human being has the ability to escape from certain limitations of his accepted mental range. Within the context of cosmo-terrestrial influences we must seek the *genius loci* – the pervading spirit of a place – which in some very old books refers to the readily perceptible energy of a particular place. In such places the current still flows today, always alive in its positive-negative bipolarity.

So, even though our doubting spirit might balk at the unknown, let us be on the side of those seekers of Life, those dynamic sceptics in search of the possible. In such a quest the true scientific spirit does not exclude imagination and meditation. On the contrary, not to call upon these qualities would be an amputation of pure research, not an enrichment.

Pascal's philosophy becomes indignant that man has "sensitivity only for the smallest things" and it asks why there is this "strange insensitivity to large concepts". This can be understood by the importance which man accords to his little ego. Also, before seeking out the power points, it seems reasonable that we should not be insensitive to what already surrounds us. First let us try to become aware of those places in our mini-environment where we feel particularly good, where we like to rest and recharge our batteries. Or, on the contrary, where we sense animosity towards us, where we feel nervous, tense, and tired.

Little by little this personal background, to which we submit unconsciously, is going to arouse our interest and permit us to discriminate between what is important and what is secondary.

By the novel approach of geobiology we will try to bridge the gap between a partial interpretation of results obtained so far and those subtle energies, waiting to be discovered or rediscovered, which – and why not? – can facilitate certain of tomorrow's scientific procedures. The name we give it is not important; along the road of evolution there is a super-structure which can accommodate a physics of the future flirting with the esoteric. The signs are undeniable.

Within the scope of our research we still lack some keys before we can break through the wall to broad daylight. Is it not precisely one role of our era to oil certain locks? Even without possessing the supreme Key, let us try to look over the barrier of the conventional world – like eager children who can no longer hold themselves back, who do not want to remain at the level of the child-man who still likes too much to play at war.

2. To have the Soul of an Explorer

We twentieth-century adults find that everything we thought we had learned leaves us with a sense of incompleteness. Have you not, perhaps when quite young, felt that subtle forces and forms existed all around you? No one ever talked about such things at school, and, alas, there was no elective course giving realistic instruction in Life with a capital "L". Still later, even with all our diplomas, and with the first flush of our exaggerated pride behind us, we doubtless caught on to the necessity of going beyond conventional technology and of doing so on our own initiative.

An escape route comes to mind: why not try to rediscover that youthful spirit and liberate in ourselves that unforeseen road to wonderment? We will then be already in contact with the vibrational energy of Life. Within the contemporary search for alternative energies, here is one form right at hand and it costs nothing! It can be a strong stimulant to the inner motive element which permits us to taste a kind of private joy, similar to the enchantment felt by that aeroplane manufacturer who always said he was astonished and full of admiration for that heavy metal body which somehow managed to stay in the air.

Or else we can retreat under the pretext of being realistic.

The essential thing is to wake up to the facts of the sensitive world, to avoid becoming locked into rigid ideas. To the degree that the frontiers of "appearance" melt away, the personality is reinforced.

Our era likes to cling to appearances. The educated world believes, for example, that it distinguishes itself by letting pass in silence Newton's predominating research in alchemy and philosophy, only bothering to refer to him in the disciplines of mathematics and physics. A falling apple was enough to create our certitudes.

3. The Ancients knew it already

These power points, called in German *Orte der Kraft*, can be defined as locations or sites endowed with an energy, a force, a strength.

This quality is related to a precise geographical location, which humans must have discovered in ancient times, whether by feeling, by intuition, by observation, or by a deep knowledge of earth-cosmos relationships which we have lost. Step by step the twentieth century has gone about rediscovering the ancient learning of those initiates called geomancers. But we must not let ourselves become intoxicated, let us not become fanatics of ancient knowledge: what was valuable in times past is not necessarily valuable today.

There is a large number of these power points on the surface of our globe. They have varying effects and some of them have been used for specific purposes. In order to find these strong spots today we have to track down, first of all, the ancient places of open-air worship, next to the temples and cathedrals, and then those tombs where corpses remain intact – as we will see later – without mummification. In these privileged locations, using appropriate means, we compare the exchange of energy between earth and sky and we seek to situate that precise spot which is most highly charged with vibrations. Will this intense point of attraction between two opposing poles create a new form of energy? Such cosmo-terrestrial interaction puts in relief the diversity of possible influences and the natural price which man will pay for his choice.

The Chinese I-Ching expresses it thus:

Heaven is the active, masculine principle, in opposition to the passive, feminine Earth. Heaven and Earth are the result of the first polarization. Penetration of the Earth by Heaven is the marriage from which is born "the Son of Heaven and Earth": Man.

In Ancient Egypt, by contrast, heaven is a feminine principle. The goddess Nut is the mother of gods and men. We will attach ourselves to this heaven in the sense of cosmic universe and to its known radiations or those in the process of becoming known.

So as to situate and assimilate as best we can the sought-for image that we are trying to illuminate and develop, it is indispensable to explain first of all just what geobiology is and what methods are used to rejuvenate this old domain left fallow.

Our approach will be standardized starting from reproducible results, without ignoring the subjective aspects. It has been possible to cross-check the convergent measurements by sophisticated instruments, principally an oscilloscope, and to relate them harmoniously with complementary data created via divination. Some marker points are sure, others mislead; some discoveries are fertile, others are sterile.

A large part of reality escapes our reasoning. However, a half-open door already admits a shaft of light, and by a chain reaction – like a flashing light projected on a crystal – it illuminates in turn the other facets. It would be wise, in any new research programme, as spectators of the invisible, to recall the attitude of Epicurus who taught us to "assert nothing, contradict nothing".

Under all latitudes the telluric current is symbolized, in one form or another, by snakes or dragons.

A Chinese allegory (below)

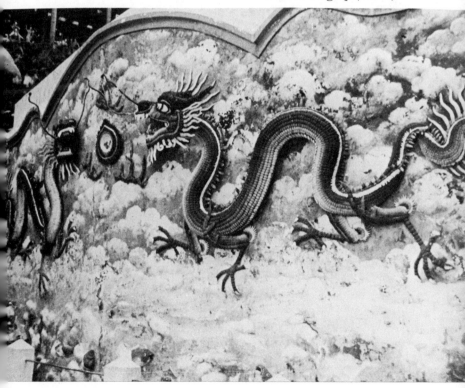

Fruit trees, growing in a Swiss orchard but above the edges of an underground stream, try to flee by leaning away from the aggressive zone.

CHAPTER 2

Geo-Earth: Its Influence on Life

1. A Little Geobiology

Geobiology is the study of the Earth's influence, at a precise point, on everything that lives, be it human, animal, or plant.

Our Earth submits to cosmic and extra-galactic radiation. It absorbs not only light rays and infra-red rays but equally a type of microwave bombardment, the origin of which is situated beyond the Milky Way.

These electromagnetic waves have a frequency modulation measured in gigahertz. Let us remember, for future reference, that a gigahertz represents one billion vibrations per second.

Our mother Earth is a living body and you can make analogies between its topography and human anatomy. A comparison with the laws of acupuncture shows preferential zones in both cases: amplified knots of energy and the meridians which correspond to terrestrial rays. Effects flow from these knots into a specific secondary network, as with the secondary meridians, and thus we come back to certain schools of thought according to whom energy flows from bottom to top.

Geobiology speaks of GEO-pathogenic penetration. Chinese acupuncture speaks of COSMO-pathogenic penetration. The same language is being used, if we admit that rays defined as terrestrial are one response to cosmic rays.

Another analogy between acupuncture and geobiology is that these terrestrial meridians, filtering through the earth's material, follow the same laws of bipolarity, of cycles, and of general systems. In the topography of the human body, and in the major meridians, what is valid for one is valid for the other. On the topography of the Earth these rivers of energy are symmetrical and equal on both hemispheres.

The terrestrial magnetic field has been revealed, in one case, by the discovery of engraving on a Breton dolmen which suggests the known spectrum of magnetic forces. In fine detail, one is struck by the resemblance of these lines to our fingerprints.

We find mention of geobiological phenomena in a Chinese-Vietnamese document which says of the above-mentioned knots that they provide a "perverse energy" which could provoke confusion in physiological functions.

Thus both the East and the West agree that a power point on the earthly crust acts as a constant, concentrated mechani-

Photographic print of microwaves radiating in the space above an underground watercourse, taken in total darkness.

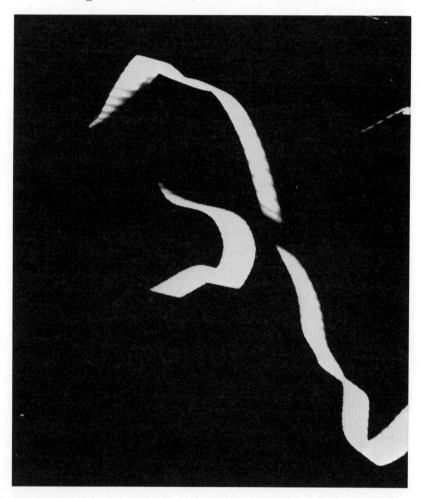

cal energy, whether beneficial or aggressive. Either effect can be suddenly swept into an accelerated rhythm.

The Hartmann network (described below) briefly sums up the Yin and Yang of ancient Chinese knowledge in a modern framework. The Yin is a cold energy which acts slowly, corresponding to winter, to north-south Hartmann rays, to cramps, and is linked to humidity and to all forms of rheumatism.

The Yang, on the other hand, is a dry, hot energy which acts rapidly. Its keyword is fire. It corresponds to the east-west H rays and is linked to inflammations.

Do not overlook the fact that a strong point, whether positive or negative, is a dynamic environment sensitive to the rhythms of the hours and the seasons.

Cosmo-terrestrial radiation will create an interaction or a transfer of energy to living matter. The rate of absorption via molecular mutation can run from several seconds to several hours, and in the course of days and years it will provoke a real cellular disequilibrium.

2. The Discovery of an Extraordinary Network

Our ancestors knew in distant times of the radiation emitted by the earth. Today there are frequent confusions in the terminology of so-called "tellurism": the influence of underground streams is mixed up with faults or with fissures of natural gas, or even with radioactivity and terrestrial magnetism, to the point that often, and justly, such collective terms are simply refused credence.

Research quickened after the end of the second world war with the discovery by a well-regarded German medical doctor, Ernst Hartmann, of a network described as telluric. This network clings to our globe in a grid pattern. Thanks to the research of this great pioneer, Dr. Hartmann, it has been possible to advance with a giant step and to grasp certain natural laws. Geobiology contributes, in particular, to widening the basis of preventive medicine as well as complementing new conceptions of the causes of disease.(★★1)

Let us mention rapidly that this Hartmann network appears as a structure of radiations rising vertically from the ground like invisible, radioactive walls, each 21 centimetres (8¼ inches) wide. From north to south they are encountered at intervals of 2 metres (6 feet, 6 inches), while from east to west they are 2.5 metres (8 feet) apart.

The dimensions of this terrestrial grille are closely akin to the mathematical roots of the pyramid of Khufu (or Cheops) – an unexpected link! (★★2) Is it only chance that at this point in the history of the earth such hidden truths emerge?

It should be specified that wherever in the H netting there is a crossing of two rays – a Hartmann knot – there is very frequently found a geopathogenic point having great import-ance for the health of a human being, even to the point of chronic illness. These are spots where one should not stay a long time, whether it be a workplace or the position of a bed. This recommendation is especially important in the case of the bed, where the physical body rests for many hours. The influence of the ground being amplified at night, it has been found that three-quarters of one's resistance is lost during sleep as compared with the waking state.

Nearly every year during the last decade someone or other "discovered" a new terrestrial system, in varieties of diagonals or horizontals, which for the most part are not orientated to the earth's magnetic field. And each of them calls himself an expert in this domain, often with the acknowledged goal of selling an apparatus protecting against harmful waves. Thus is serious research prejudiced.

Geobiology is equally interested in the influence of water on the health and chronic fatigue of individuals. It has been confirmed in a general way that underground water serves to amplify the Hartmann network.

It goes without saying that geobiology does not ignore the positive aspects of this element as a source of life, as a medium of purification and renewal.

In India water is as sacred as the Prana, the breath of life. Without water, the nomadic peoples would quickly dis-appear. Do not let rain put you in a bad humour; it is a blessing.

According to Dr. Hartmann the network forms a vast invisible whole, like a precisely-woven net spread over the entire surface of the globe.

Remember that this gridwork is magnetically orientated: from north to south one of these "invisible walls" occurs

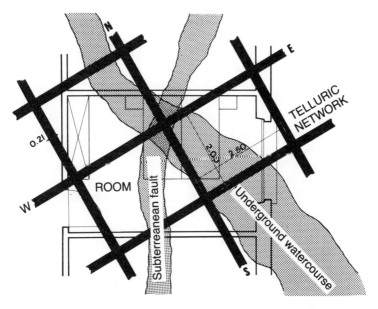

Position of a bed disturbed by a geopathic zone. Cumulated effect of a telluric crossing-point, a fault, and a subterranean watercourse.

every 2 metres (6 feet, 6 inches) and from east to west the interval is 2.5 metres (8 feet, 2 inches). Between these geometric lines lies a neutral zone, an unperturbed micro-climate. The characteristic width of the lines is 21 centimetres (just over 8 inches). This network penetrates everywhere, whether over open ground or through dwellings.

In order to understand these phenomena it has been necessary to study the fields of geophysics, geology, hydro-logy, even microbiology and bioelectronics.

3. Well Being linked to the Dwelling

We have known for a long time that when there is water under a dwelling, whether an underground stream or an important water table, the inhabitants always feel more tired than on neutral ground. Premature ageing and a loss of vitality can often be confirmed.

These geological anomalies can be measured on the surface; on the edges of watercourses the microwaves have an electrochemical potential higher than in the centre. By other measurements a reduction of thermic neutron radiation, coming from the great depths of the earth's crust, is shown. Here we touch the domain of atomic physics.

Other reports reveal an ionization of the earth discharging its heat, measurable by infra-red, an ionization whose intensity diminishes above a watercourse.

To demonstrate the terrestrial effect on human beings, we can cite the excellent georhythmogram as one of the best reproducible tests. Using an ohmmeter and two electrodes to measure the individual's skin resistance, we get a clear indication, in kilo-ohms, if the person is aggressed or not by a given environment.

Geocancerology has already accumulated a thick file of data: the fatal effect is present when a bed is located over a crossing-point of the Hartmann network, amplified by the presence of subterranean water. Cells located on a geopathogenic point become tired or, contrarily, defend themselves by multiplying.

Dr. Hartmann demonstrated, in other circumstances, that a patient who sleeps with a telluric knot under the stomach loses hydrochloric acid.

The candidate for a heart attack is frequently found where the workplace is located over an H crossing, a condition repeated at night in bed if the heart is also directly over a knot. There is no lack of examples of the "elected" between 37 and 42 years of age; stress gets the blame. There are spectacular cases among children suffering from insomnia, even with prescription tranquillizers; they sleep and thrive once their little bed is moved to a neutral zone. The nightmare situation of the bedwetter gives way to a blossoming-out once the bed is moved.

Where underground water seeps upward through the walls of a house by capillary action, one can observe that the nearby trees are covered with moss, with mould, with grubs – understand by this the danger of larvate diseases such as rheumatism, cramps, etc.

Thus, while water coursing under a habitation is to be avoided, by contrast a stream situated nearby and open to the sky will favourably discharge the electrical environment.

The art of building a healthful house is not covered in

these pages; such is a separate subject for which specialized books exist. The important thing for the house and the householder is not to get boxed into a state of biological limbo, such as with air-conditioning for example.

Treatment of illness is crowned with success in 70 per cent of the cases, with hardly any relapses, where the family doctor takes account of the discoveries made through geobiology. Insurance companies – and all the sectors which wail about the rising cost of health – will not long remain indifferent to such factors.

We are millions of fragile beings.

The place of recuperation and silence, the most important place for the individual, should be the bedroom.

The site of the bed, it must be repeated, plays a paramount role. It is a parameter which must not be neglected. It is there that the physical and mental forces must be able to rebuild the vital forces essential to the next day. The bed is also the symbol of regeneration in sleep and in love; it is usually a bed which welcomes the human being at birth and which listens to his last breath of life.

4. The H Network predicts Weather and Earthquakes

The Earth's body signals its internal shiverings by the expression of a dynamic energy which varies according to the hours, the rhythms of the seasons and according to the play of the planets in the celestial spray.

Weather
Twenty-four hours before the arrival of an atmospheric low pressure zone we observe a 100 per cent increase of gamma rays on the knots of the Hartmann grid, and on volcanic soil the increase may be up to 300 per cent. This concentrated radioactivity spurts from the earth at that precise spot, in such a violent way that individuals already unconsciously sensitized to the influence of that spot will feel a strong worsening of their ailments. These indications translate, on the psychological plane, into a real depression. The evidence unfortunately confirms this to be the moment of real crisis, even suicide.

In the same way, the electrical field of the atmosphere charges up to 50 kHz before a storm. The human being becomes more and more tense until the moment the rain begins to fall. Then a charge of ± 4000 volts per metre drops suddenly by 50 to 500 volts per metre, thus reducing the surcharge of positive ions. By comparison, the calm of good weather measures about 100 volts per metre. It is interesting to note that a lightning bolt generally has a diameter of about one metre.

It is curious to register, using the automatic georhythmo-gram during the approach of a storm, a difference of sensitivity between people of the black race and those of the white race. The former, in a room completely blacked-out to the light and insulated against outside noise, with the eyes blindfolded, exhibit startle responses to each stroke of lightning produced by a storm still a great distance away. But whites remain rather indifferent to everything that occurs during solar eruptions, eclipses of the sun and the moon, magnetic storms, and volcanic bubblings.

At Essen there is a centre of information for doctors who want advice on weather fluctuations. Effects on the human being are studied within the framework of bio-meteorology.

Variations in radioactivity
Dr. Hartmann kept measuring apparatus in operation day and night for several years, simultaneously logging neutral zones and telluric knots. He reports there is a sag in the Earth's natural radioactivity every afternoon about five o'clock.

The Max Planck Institute in West Germany has found, within the context of biophysical research, that microwaves have a strong influence on blood and tissue. The result for humanity is a loss of energy potential, even depolarization.

Is this the time of day when some of us feel tired, in response to this weakening of radiation, and reach instinctively for a stimulant – coffee, a cigarette?

Could it be that the custom of five o'clock tea was born of a need to adapt naturally to this daily rhythm?

At our latitudes a Geiger-Muller counter registers a normal background radioactivity of 20 microroentgens per hour within the neutral zone of the H network. One

measures an average increase of 30 per cent on the intersections.

Above Celtic tombs and above caverns where animals
have been preserved the reading is 30 to 40 per cent higher
than average. At the power points which we are now going
to visit the Hartmann crossing-points show up to 50 per
cent increased radioactivity.

Forecasting earthquakes
Through the discovery of the H network it is possible to
foresee an earthquake 12 hours in advance, somewhere on
the globe, but for the moment it is not yet within our power
to pinpoint it geographically.

Let us remember that a Hartmann ray has a "thickness"
of 21 centimetres (9 inches). When the first contractions and
dilations commence deep within the Earth's crust, we find
that the ray's width has tripled. This thickening can be
interpreted in the following way:

The known Hartmann ray is formed of a central ray
accompanied on its right and on its left by two secondary
rays of weaker intensity, these not being detectable under
normal or "calm" ground conditions. When an earthquake
is brewing, the intensity of these adjoining secondary lines
becomes equal to that of the principal ray. Could it not be
this anomaly that animals feel and which causes them to
flee?

At these times dogs howl to high heaven, birds flutter
madly in their cages, certain cats hide under the quilt on the
bed, and certain people – yes – feel sick or suddenly have a
great need to sleep.

We are all more or less antennae, relatively simple
receivers.

At the instant and on the site of an earthquake we find that
the H network is knocked topsy-turvy: the lines are twisted
and curved, but a half-hour later the system is back in place.
The Earth's crust has its nervous system; by analogy we
have our own, but after a good shock ours requires more
time to recuperate.

These earthquake forecasts are valid only when it is a
matter of our Earth breathing by all its pores. The H
network also permits distinguishing a natural earthquake
from a shock that has been provoked, a cataclysm deliber-

ately organized by the destructive human brain. Alas, there are these insane underground nuclear explosions which mangle the H network – sometimes for several days – and in such cases Nature gives no warning!

5. *Observing Power Points: Methodology*

In examining this relationship of Earth to Man (even Earth-Man-Cosmos on the power points), the telluric network reveals unexpected situations, confirming our presence on no simple, run-of-the-mill boundary line.

At first we believed it possible to place our faith entirely in the most sophisticated equipment offered by modern technology. As a technologist seeking to be objective and rational, your geobiologist has used, according to the situation, high frequency detectors, the 308S oscillograph, shortwave receivers equipped with microammeters, magnetometers with proton resonance, ohmmeters, the Geiger-Muller counter, electrofiltration current receivers, a scintillation counter, and other similar instrumental delicacies.

Through a feeling of respect for certain sites, it was not possible to deploy all such equipment. So, in the long run, we limited ourselves to the following three methods:
  – the Geiger counter for site radioactivity;
  – the lobe wand for situating the Hartmann network;
  – the Bovis biometer for measuring site intensity.

Some experienced researchers have declared the latter two, the lobe antenna and the Bovis biometer, to be indispensable although more subjective in application. It is wise, however, to remain attentive to the interpretation which one gives to a result, even when a purely mechanical instrument duplicates a measurement involving some subjectivity.

So it is that we have been able to approach these focal points using the Geiger counter, the lobe wand, and the Bovis biometer.

Encouraged by a team of well-known scientists, we have been audacious enough to add divination to this last method, although some circles tolerate it only with a certain disdain. It has however the merit of being a method suitably discreet for studying sacred places. In the French language divining is called "radiesthésie", a term which is derived from the Latin "radius" – "ray" in English – and the Greek "aisthesis" – meaning "sensation".

The biometer conceived by the physicist Bovis and the engineer Simoneton is a sort of calibrated scale or ruler on which the pendulum can indicate the intensity of a spot. The authors of this biometer have selected for the scale, and quite rightly, wave lengths known in physics, such as the colour red corresponding to 6500 Angstroms. One Å = one 10-millionth of a millimetre.

Other researchers have preferred to express it in frequency, such as the Gigahertz. One Gigahertz = one billion vibrations per second. To facilitate our comparisons we will remain aloof from these terms and will cite our results in units without labels. When all is said and done these are simply units of an effect.

It was the cathedral of Chartres which touched off our curiosity. We were surprised by the number of units of effect which exceeded the norms known until then. This first survey created a benchmark for comparisons with other sites, particularly in India, Egypt, Santiago de Compostela, and a Himalayan plateau.

Thus another window of geobiological information opened, allowing confirmation that these energy foci were not situated at such-and-such a place simply by chance.

6. The Three Dimensions of the Biometer

In view of the abundant esoteric literature of recent years, brimming with confusing overlaps, it is necessary to stick to a standard terminology when interpreting the scale of values on the Bovis meter.

The knowledge of universal laws which we are trying to penetrate reaches deeply into antiquity. In any case contemporary man, caught in a veritable tornado of computers, finds pleasure in conceiving of the existence of intangible entities.

As for the terminology to adopt, it should be clear and uniformly used, but we are blocked at the level of squabbling children. An example of frequently differing interpretations is the word "Aura", used willy-nilly with meanings differing widely according to the appreciations of various authors. It would be desirable that this Aura, a luminous mist, not be confused with the radiation of the etheric or energizing body which we are trying to locate through measurements in the second segment of the biometer.

With the illumination to be brought by tomorrow's scientific developments, these ancient and subjective techniques will become, without doubt, more and more refined. Yet, in spite of all the perfection of future instrumentation, intuitive Man will have to remain the centre, the Initiator.

For us, the three dimensions of the biometer are:

Sector no. 1, the *physical*, going from 0 to 10,000 units, giving the intensity of the site, the vibration having an effect on the physical human being.

Sector no. 2, one passes beyond Bovis's conception and penetrates into the domain of the energizing body, also known as the *etheric* body; the biometer reads from 11,000 to 13,500 units.

Sector no. 3, ranges from 13,500 to 18,000 units; it penetrates subtly into the *spiritual* domain and into a secret universe which one measures in sanctuaries, up to the rare levels of initiation.

Sector no. 4 is at the threshold of the Unknown; such was the exceptional case of Compostela.

Development and Analysis of our System of Approach

1. From 0 to 10,000 units on the scale

A site in average equilibrium from the point of view of intensity, without major disturbance, without supplemental energy as well, hence neutral, registers 6500 units.

Below this figure the environment is weakened and can become noxious for man, animal or plant. It falls generally to 2000 on an intersection of the Hartmann network.

When the effect of a place is improved, whether by eliminating nuisances or by modifying the oscillating circuit, it should give between 7500 and 8000 units.

A reading of 9000 is already too violent for human beings, at least over the long term. A georhythmogram will show agitated curves.

By way of comparison these values can be applied to the human being as follows: 6500 units is the level of normal vitality; moving up to 7000 or 8000 units we reach our full vital energy.

Everything that we have been able to establish so far allows us to confirm that humanity, on average, is not very well!

We find that the person whose vitality falls to 3000 or 2000 units will be very sick, and with only 1000 units he has one foot in the grave. Bear in mind that the geopathogenic Hartmann or telluric knot registers only 2000 units.

This first sector of the biometer corresponds to the site or to the physical body, thus to matter that is dense.

In this first sector the instrument indicates, for a place, the cosmo-telluric activity. For man it shows the energy of his body of flesh, the carrier for the etheric and spiritual bodies.

2. From 11,000 to 13,500 units on the scale

In this range we measure the quality of the energizing, etheric body. It can be described as an invisible envelope around the physical body, imperceptible to the naked eye but revealed by Kirlian electrophotography. The Kirlian process causes the energizing body to be outlined by luminous colours, ranging from blue flame to scarlet red. There are nuances in the tones and intensities according to whether the subject is healthy or unwell.

This is precisely what some claim to see as the aura, but the aura should not be confused and compared to the etheric body. This latter, whose emanation is from one to three centimetres (about 1 inch) thick around the physical body, moulds itself perfectly around the physical form and is, so to speak, its double. Russian savants speak, in this case, of a dematerialized form of organic plasma, or bio-plasma.

The Kirlian effect or other similar procedures provide supplemental help in detecting the influence of a physical environment on the human being. The results brought forward are quite different according to whether the person is living in an air-conditioned building of steel and concrete or is lodged in a house of brick or wood.

Useless to specify which one is the closest to Nature!

One is equally surprised in these procedures to observe modifications of the etheric body according to mood: we have only to compare intensity and luminosity of this second body before and after a meditation!

This "second skin" contains vitality and basic energy which is transferred to the physical body by close interaction; it is like a fluid fabric or force lines and light. It is also known that this vital force, slumbering in our centres of consciousness, the chakras, animates the etheric body and this in turn nourishes the physical body.

Energizing body and etheric body – these are two terms for a single reality.

Certain cures obtained only by treating the energizing body can thus be understood. Re-establishing the integrity of this etheric cover, by "plugging" any gaps, will act by projection on the physical disorder, on this dense body which will obey like a robot.

These two bodies, physical and energizing, are as one so long as the human being is incarnate; both are doomed to death, but they do not necessarily disappear at the same time! Observations made to this effect, during the separation between a physical vehicle and its subtle body, are reported in the last chapter.

This etheric body is also the zone which focuses all the form of manifest life, capturing planetary, solar and cosmic influences. Everything is linked.

So it is that we even register the effect of these interactions in the forms of emotion, suffering or joy. And all that is translated into the physical body as a stimulation or as a brake, even resonating as a mental blockage.

A disturbed dwelling or other place will serve to amplify an existing feeling of general discomfort. In contrast, a well-balanced body will be capable of fighting intelligently against invasion and disruption of health by calling upon its reserves.

Within the framework of orthodox medicine the existence and the function of the etheric body is only partially acknowledged. However, this same medicine offers in the pharmaceutical marketplace a variety of vitamin products aimed at greater vitality and reinforcement of the energy circuit. Interaction over and over again, this working on the densest organ to lighten a mood . . . is it not said that the way to a man's heart is through his stomach?

This second dimension on the Bovis scale relates to physical subtleties which are not less metaphysical.

3. From 13,500 to 18,000 units on the scale

One had better be well trained in order to dare confront this third dimension through mental means. We follow the same rhythm and the same principle of measurement, but sometimes we are flirting with dizzy heights. If you want to know the composition of a candle it is not certain you will be able to analyse the flame. This third dimension permits, however, a more comprehensive understanding of the impact of an energy focal point and its influence on the human being. It is possible, referring back to the preceding levels of the biometer, to place cosmic and spiritual impulses side by side with those that are purely physical and etheric – the latter serving in turn as a metaphysical relay and a subtle support for currents coming from higher spheres.

In order to establish a contact on a sacred site, we must liberate ourselves from sterilizing limitations and hook on to what one could call higher minds. This is sometimes a highwire exercise.

It can happen that on a very precise point of cosmo-telluric convergence, in a place of consecration where the biometer gives an intensity of 18,000 units – meaning a place where only an Initiate has the ability to remain in this field of sublime force – the simple mortal who stumbles in unawares sometimes receives these combined impulses in a violent form. He risks becoming unhinged in all three bodies that we have just described.

This experience can at the same time also provoke an illumination. Lack of awareness is not always an obstacle.

Certain of our intellectuals have established the existence of a scale of seven bodies. Let them be reassured: it is not an oversight that we are going to limit ourselves voluntarily to the three bodies cited above. They are sufficient for investigations into these focal points of cosmo-telluric energy. We will place to one side the astral body which can escape during sleep, so that we can explore a more down-to-earth universe. With part of this baggage we will now visit some of the world's spiritual centres.

CHAPTER 3

Egypt

1. Lines of Force

Between the wide meanderings of the Nile and the sterility of the desert there are, in what remains of Ancient Egypt, several power points which deserve to be "X-rayed" through a geobiologist's eyes. The great lines of force gradually emerge and one can only stand in awe of that immense Knowledge, in part lost today.

The famous pyramid of Cheops, or Khufu, is, without any doubt, a pyramid of initiation, even if some of the guides do not want to be bothered with distinguishing it from the other pyramid-tombs. The so-called sarcophagus which is found in the middle of the king's high-ceilinged chamber is a rectangular vat of such small size that it could not hold a human body, even if this latter had been curled up in its original embryonic position. One might imagine that, for the initiation canditate reaching this place after many tests, this vat could symbolically represent the ultimate receptacle of the power of life and metamorphosis. He will have endured a symbolic death and in returning to Earth he will feel liberated from negative and regressive forces. He will no longer be of his body, he will simply use it. After having wooed death he will no longer be the same as before, he will see the face of the world with other eyes. The hero who will have experienced this initiatory path will have to have penetrated, to reach this focal point of Egyptian initiation, the strangling constriction of a low, narrow passage where one grovels, crawls, withdraws into the self – a sort of dis-creation, like a grain of wheat buried in the ground before evolving to another dimension.

One may be puzzled by this ritual and by that possibility of being "born again" which our churches are trying to make us understand in a mental way. It really seems as if it is always necessary to die a little in order to experience renewal.

O pyramid of Khufu, you have been partially pulled down, and your blocks have been re-used, with their polarities reshuffled in total anarchy, to build the mosque of Sultan Hassan in Cairo.

How powerful you were when you could still function as a magnet to the initiatory forces of the land; how beautiful must have been the illumination on your face at the dawn of the equinox, signalling to distant peoples the time to sow and the time to reap.

All the mystic geography of Ancient Egypt was decreed according to the fourteen parts of Osiris's mutilated body, the fourteen vital centres of the country: its power points still topical. We are not going to repeat here all the figures, all the calculations known and widely disseminated through the writings specializing in this tri-unity which are the pyramids. Our geobiological study teaches us that these gigantic Pharaonic structures have this in common: the Hartmann network forms a veritable dam of 18 geomagnetic lines around the perimeter of the buildings. The visitor who tries to cross this barrier, insofar as he is reasonably sensitive, will feel them as a brake, as an invisible obstacle. In circling such a building without straying from the lines in question, he begins to drag his feet. They feel heavier and heavier and seem to be glued to the ground.

This type of obstructive and protective belt surrounding these giants is as detectable around the Great Pyramid as around the pyramids sheltering tombs, such as the terraced pyramid of Saqqarah where lies Ptah, patron of the artisans of Memphis. And one discovers the same phenomenon around the celebrated temples of Luxor, Karnak, Thebes and Kawn Umbu, as well as in the Valley of Kings around two tombs with less protection: around the one where Narth lies and, curiously, around the tomb of Chamuas there are only seven H ray barrier lines instead of 18. This latter sepulchre was restored in 1903 by an Italian archeological mission – why is there a different density? Did the restoration modify the site, or is there a formula relating to the youth of the deceased, who was only ten years old?

The question arises whether these lines of the Hartmann network, condensed outside the walls as if to protect them, are not absent in the interior of the building. And that is just what we can confirm everywhere: the telluric gridwork is

The 18 lines of the Hartmann network form a real barrier before the great temples and around the pyramids.

pushed back toward the edges of the structure in such a way that the interior enjoys an immense neutral zone, free of H rays!

These ancient temples have several spacious rooms, separated by imposing walls of a thickness going up to two metres. The large openings and the interior passages have very wide thresholds traversed, in every case, by seven tightly-packed Hartmann rays, creating a kind of brake. The unaware visitor will not feel them any more than the beam of light opening our modern automatic doors.

But in the distant ages which have left us these majestic vestiges, man did not penetrate with our brisk pace. The passage invited him to halt, to meditate, encouraging his preparation for crossing the next threshold.

This number 7 will always declare itself where there is a concentration of force lines, whether in Egypt or, as we shall see farther on, at Chartres and at Santiago de Compostela. Additionally, this number seven is often cited: it indicates the passage from known to unknown, the completion of a cycle.

It corresponds to 7 days in the week and to the 7 planets known to ancient man. There are the 7 stars in Ursa Major, the 7 metals, the 7 colours of the rainbow. In the Bible, the Pharaoh dreams of 7 fat cows and 7 lean cows. Without dwelling too much on this, it is still interesting to recall the 7 towers of Mecca where the pilgrim must make 7 turns around the Kaaba; the 7 branches of the Hebrew candelabra which acts as a regulator of vibrations; and the 7 degrees of perfection which permit passage from Earth to Heaven, this idea being preserved in the funeral text of the Book of the Dead.

The great number of Pharaonic temples along the Nile certainly have a common language, but each one develops its own theme individually.

In the imposing atmosphere of Ancient Egypt, tracking the sources of the universal religion, it is gripping to juxtapose the measurements of the H network with the biometer. This is a new way to follow the life paths of the Pharaohs and the initiated priests; this kind of Egyptology takes a vibratory leap.

So we advance under the Egyptian sky, symbolized by the goddess Nut of the curved body; she swallowed the sun each evening and gave it rebirth early the next morning. She held her arched figure off the ground with her fingertips. But we are going to approach on tiptoe . . .

2. Aswan Dam chased away the Good Spirits

We have more and more the conviction that the sites of these ancient temples were not chosen blindly.

In the original temples, that is to say, those which have not been displaced by construction of the Aswan Dam, we still discover the same signs. It turns out that the structures

Always 7 Hartmann rays on the wide thresholds . . . you are invited to stop, to prepare the next passage.

which were dismantled and carefully reconstructed on another site still present the same visible architecture – but it is finished, it is no longer a power point, there is no more *genius loci*!

Let us take a concrete example, the temple of Isis at Philae, saved from the waters of the dam. Its orientation is north-south, although the other old temples direct their principal façades to the south-east. On its new emplacement there is no longer a frontal rank of 18 force lines barring the way. The gridwork of the telluric network is quite regular without any whim. There are not the 7 lines guarding the thresholds between interior passages, such as are found in all the other temples left on their original sites. Only the statutes at the entrance have kept their original vibrations, with 9000 units on the positive side and 2000 on the negative side.

The stones destined for the reconstruction of the temple of Isis had been carefully marked, yet even the engineer who was responsible for this monumental jigsaw acknowledged, once the job was done, that he was a little disappointed: "It is no longer the same".

The gigantic Aswan Dam or Lake Nasser stretches upstream for 500 kilometres (310 miles) and is 4 kilometres (2.5 miles) wide. It is the new symbol of modern times. It creates nevertheless so much evaporation that the blue and luminous skies of yesteryear have given way to permanently cloudy skies. If the dam should be damaged – one dare not think of it – waves sixty metres high would rampage over 1000 kilometres and wipe Egypt from the map of the world.

3. Who is Responsible: The Site or the Architect?

Until now we have had to leave open the question of whether a power point has been selected with respect to a known telluric network, before construction, or whether such a large neutral zone, such as are found inside these edifices, develops after the fact as an emission of the shape deliberately calculated by constructor-initiates. Doubtless Egypt herself could provide an answer if certain of her temples could be removed. For even though on the new sites the telluric concentrations and the captive affinities are no longer found, and the place has lost its influence in this domain, to our great astonishment the interior neutral zone has reconstituted itself.

Do we dare affirm that the dimensions and the waves of structural forms play a considerable role in the built environment? From that can we pose this question: does not the architect carry a certain, if not sacred, responsibility in this domain, yesterday and today?

This kind of proposal may stimulate future builders and

allow them to find a new and fascinating orientation for creating harmonious interiors and dwellings.

"Architecture is also philosophy, otherwise construction limits itself to a simple technique of piling one brick on another", such is the verdict of an old Egyptian builder.

Thus it seems we can submit the thesis that a power point combines two aspects of influence: both the site and the context of the structure.

A room too high, out of proportion with its width, already makes an impact on the human being. One can find places, used in ancient times for magic, where one feels crushed, blocked, lost.

Curiously, and not mischievously, we find similar disproportionate dimensions in a renowned high chamber, none other than the senatorial hall of the Council of States in the Swiss capitol at Berne.

Coming back to the question of emissions related to shape: all supporting elements carry a more subtle form, reflecting the human body. The temple columns support also the consciousness of the site: the square bases symbolizing knowledge, the rounded columns alluding to love. Is not that a happy marriage of reason?

It is fortunate that new interdisciplinary options are emerging, after the manner of our great educational institutions. In the wheel of progress the cycles of advance and regression are inevitable.

Today's geobiology could be a bridge of conciliation between architecture and medicine. It is interesting to remark that the ancient Egyptians, such as Imhotep, elevated to be the god of medicine, had actually fulfilled two roles in life: he was both doctor and architect at the court of King Djoser of the Third Dynasty, about 3000 years before Christ.

We want to develop a real science of the dwelling and the workplace which is more humane and more real.

The reply to our question – who is responsible, the site or the architect? – must be: both of them are.

4. Their Bricks were not Sterile

In the building of a house, brick followed closely the use of earth (clay, adobe). It became the means of protection for a clan and turned the wandering nomads into a sedentary society. It fixed man in place, in his residence and in his tomb; doubtless these archaic structures possessed high vibratory qualities.

Today these same bricks are hardened around a rigid, static framework, suffocating any vital exchange. Man has been put in a cage from the moment of building several stories high; complaints about the assault on human dignity arise wherever there is excess.

It was necessary to evolve from brick to stone in order to raise those monumental structures that we still admire in Egypt. Stone was extracted from within the internal mass of the quarry and never from the outside, where it had been attacked by erosion. The polarization of the stone and the brick played an important role in the ritual of laying the foundations of temples. This care and respect for the polarity of the material already began in the quarry, in obedience to very old rules and traditions. The raw stone was considered to be androgynous; the stone cut, the two characteristics separated.

Inside the temples one finds that positive polarities have been placed on the outside and the negative polarities are turned toward the interior. Without doubt, this way of building permitted a natural neutralization of disturbing effects in the environment. The illiterate would say that it would never be noticed, however we know that the Egyptians observed a correlation between north polarity and the positive, west, red, autumn and drought; south polarity corresponded to the negative, east, white, sunrise and springtime.

Better yet, the propitious day for laying the first stone was chosen according to planetary indications and the sacred book of the builders was consulted. Nothing was left to chance at the opening of a building site. The principles of cosmic harmony designated even the material and the quarry from which it should be extracted.

These builders possessed a sensitivity to the influences in the stone. They believed that, the soul of a rock being weak, a large mass of stones selected from one specific place would become a collective force, inseparable from the sacred spirit of the ground on which it was assembled.

It is interesting to find, even today, that stones and bricks revealing these two polarities have been used for the construction of farm houses in that region. These bricks are still made by hand and fired in proximity to the dwellings. Do these peasants still know how to lay polarities as their ancestors did? Obviously we cannot ask our industries to juggle such subtleties, but a certain amount of observation and individual attention would at least show a welcome departure from our routine frame of reference.

Thanks to the geological structure of Egypt and its red granite, even the unobservant visitor will feel a stimulation of energy measuring up to 9000 units. This is especially noticeable in Upper Egypt where the granitic mass rises to the surface.

5. Harmony and Violence at Luxor

According to Schwaller de Lubicz the foundation plans of the temple of Amenhotep III at Luxor, called the Temple of Man, recapitulate the complete bone structure of a human skeleton. It is situated in a special enclosure where the body of Man is the temple, place of divine intervention.

Interested by this juxtaposition, we measured the vitality of the site. As an example and for comparison, we found 6500 biometer units in the centre of the temple, which corresponds exactly to the vibrations of man's solar plexus. The following measurements were always found to be in relation to the human form. Walking to the level of the head, on the sacred spot of Naos or the third eye, one is surprised that the highest vibration rises to 18,000 units. This is the point where there is nothing more of the physical, nor of the etheric, but only the pure spiritual vibration.

This emplacement was destined only for the Pharaoh and his priest-initiates. Even today such a powerful vibration does not permit us to stop there; the spot is too violent. Do not forget that initiates arrived there after long preparation, a gradual gearing-up of their own vibrations to successively higher levels, so as to be consciously able to adapt to and support the divine vibration. It is a slow walk, a rigorous ritual, going up from the square in front of the feet of the symbolic Man, traversing the body of the Temple up to the tabernacle. One must not be astonished if, in such a power

point, the visitor without mystical experience feels rather uncomfortable!

6. *Hathor's Fainting Lovers*

The most evident demonstration of geobiology having been applied in distant times is revealed in the temple of Hathor at Dandarah, named after the goddess of love called Aphrodite by the Greeks. On this Egyptian focal point there are four subterranean watercourses all around the temple. They are so well directed into regular canals that it could not be a natural phenomenon, but deliberate.

These channels intersect in the four corners around the temple. The crossing of forces and the force of the crossing is not discovered only in geobiology. This concept is found across the whole of Pharaonic thought and is elaborated on a universal principle, whether applied to mathematics or in medicine.

At one corner of the temple of Hathor the waters are gathered into the sacred lake. Artificial lakes were almost always dug near temples and became their "liquid heaven". Nocturnal mysteries were performed on their shores, and priests accomplished their ritual ablutions in these waters.

Two watercourses run from the other side under a gate only four metres square and here there are two sets of 7 tightly-packed Hartmann rays, intersecting to produce the effect of a menhir. This geophysical concentricity is of such violence that the uninformed stroller is immediately seized with discomfort or flees. There exist several of these points specifically on the edges and in the interiors of the Egyptian foci. Once you have discovered these spots, it is amusing to observe nonchalant tourists who, on reaching one, commence to fidget, or feel oppressed even to the point of fainting. One should not believe that it is a question of sorcery or the evil eye, as is often said. We can now depend on other parameters.

All around this great temple are found, as always, the 18 lines of the Hartmann network which provide a protective barrier.

The entrance to the Temple of Man at Luxor, such as it appears to the visitor today.

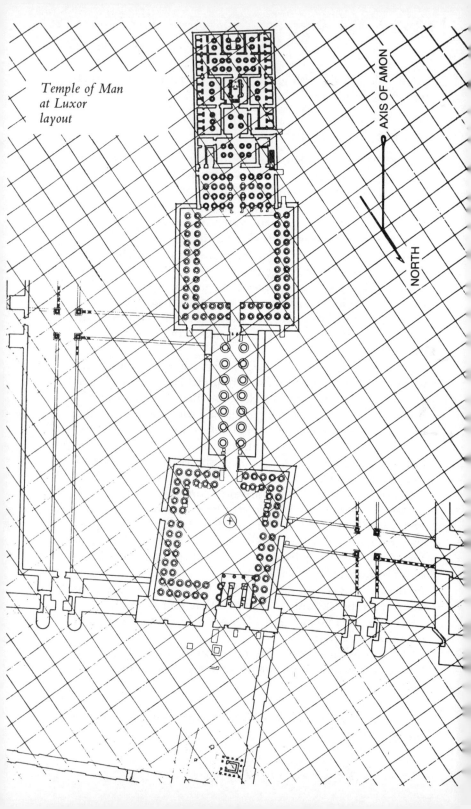

Temple of Man at Luxor layout

AXIS OF AMON

NORTH

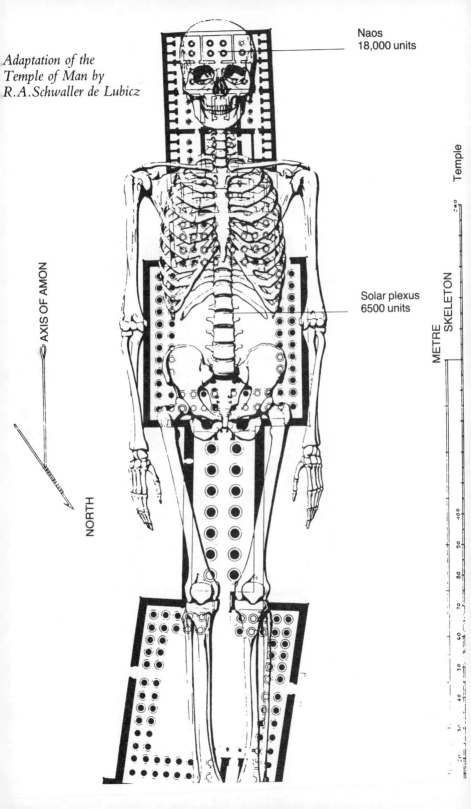

Adaptation of the
Temple of Man by
R.A.Schwaller de Lubicz

Naos
18,000 units

Solar plexus
6500 units

AXIS OF AMON

NORTH

Temple

METRE   SKELETON

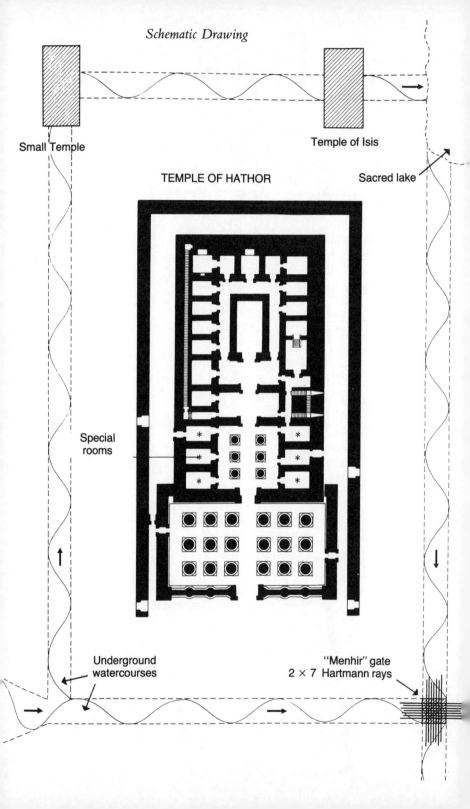

Schematic Drawing

Small Temple

Temple of Isis

TEMPLE OF HATHOR

Sacred lake

Special
rooms

Underground
watercourses

"Menhir" gate
2 × 7 Hartmann rays

Nearby there is a little temple which was the birthplace of Isis and where, under the solar disk decorating the ceiling, a vibration of 10,000 units is found. Under the solar disk of the temple of Hathor, in contrast, the vibration goes up to 16,000 units and seems to be very powerful.

Within the same architectural complex there is a small temple-hospital where women came to give birth under the protection and blessing of the goddess Beth. There are no particular signs here; it is quite without fanfare.

Magic in the lateral chapels
On both sides of the temple there are three lateral rooms, noted on the sketch, which must have been used for the practice of magic. The same architectural layout is also found at Abydos. After we have stood still for a moment in these places our skin absorbs this special atmosphere, and whoever is able to keep a cool head will observe that his thoughts are troubled. In these rooms the Hartmann network shows wildly tightened links in all directions, and our biometer falls under 1000 units. The same phenomenon occurs in front of the statues of the goddess Sekhmet; it is a vibrational level which corresponds to that of the passage of death or nothingness.

If your curiosity is stimulated, you can try to stay on your feet as long as possible in these places, where you will feel that a sort of invisible presence is taking over and will try to make you lose your lucidity, to draw you into an energy pit the better to disorient you.

An inhabitant of the area would never set foot in the place. At most he will remain at the entrance, following you with an indefinable expression where fear and disapproval are mixed.

If these moods can already be provoked by the power of the place and the waves of shapes, then we can hardly imagine what a human being might feel in a state of ritual exaltation! In these rooms the biometer makes impressive leaps: there are certain points which, with 11,000 units, give the feeling of weightlessness. Some of the walls are decorated with compelling paintings where there are, according to the subject, enormous disparities in the vibrations. To cite a concrete example: in front of the image of the phoenix there are only a weak 1000 units, but before a magic hand which plunges a snake in a bowl, the biometer confirms an insupportable vibration oscillating up to 20,000 units. These decorations represent the Neters; they are the principles, the natural forces of the Egyptian cosmogony. Here we find ourselves in zones of influences where physical laws, such as we know them, no longer play a determining role. The currents which impregnate these places seem to have remained intact across the ages.

7. Fleeting Figures, Immortal Influences

A stroll between the sphinx heads lining the grand avenue, which in its time linked Karnak to Luxor, will bring a beneficial effect. There are places and objects, and even trees, which exhibit energies and emissions due to their shapes and which can enter into resonance with our own cells.

This wide avenue, bordered with superb ram's-head sphinxes, will restore your equilibrium simply if you walk down and back again. Here we confirm that the "plus" or positive polarities are found in front of the sphinx heads, facing the visitor. The biometer confirms a physical vibration higher than 9500 units. Additionally, there is a vibratory emission which touches the etheric body at its maximum tolerance of 13,500 units. The faithful should walk to the temple of Luxor at a slow pace permitting concentration, so as to become thoroughly impregnated with these emissions. It would doubtless be profitable for a visitor to make this round trip in the old-fahioned way, without hurrying.

Let us not forget the Great Sphinx of Giza who, for long centuries, has contemplated with his enigmatic stare the coming of dawn. He must be hiding within him the secrets of humanity or the Hidden Way of Knowledge. He is a powerful guardian who doubtless promises some deeply moving discoveries, when the time comes to unveil the access to the secret door. For the moment, under his motionless eyes, he offers known vibrations ranging only between 8000 and 13,500 – so he is still of this world.

It is at Tel-el-Amarna that one of the largest statues in the history of humanity is found. This site is the birthplace and the wellspring of the first universal religion. It is here that

Akhenaton, Pharaoh of the Eighteenth Dynasty, proclaimed 3500 years ago the Deus Unicus, the one God. The temple of Akhenaton is carved in a mountain of this desert. The sensitive visitor will find the sun painted on the wall of this power point, where the solar rays are tipped with hands transmitting life and light. Here we measure a calm and beneficial energy of 8000 units. The modern human being will be more, or less, conscious of it according to his degree of evolution.

On the spot where the priest stands we find 11,000 units, the same number of vibrations as in the cathedral of Chartres. Akhenaton glorified the sun, the Light of the One God, and the joy of living.

This first cry for one single religion under one single consciousness was uttered fifteen centuries before Jesus Christ, and today we are trying to speak the same language. With our Gospels we are the readers of a library inspired by Judaism; each of them remains locked into its form of individual belief, although in divine reality there is no difference between Allah and God.

The beautiful Nefertiti was Akhenaton's inspiration. She is spoken of little, but her charm and distinction have traversed the centuries. This face is not fleeting, thanks to the numerous artists who have immortalized her features.

The universal dialogue in the direction of Unity continues. Although the divinities of Ancient Egypt have vanished, let us not forget that it was the old country of the Nile which harboured the first antenna of this message. But the evolution of man's spirit is slow.

8. Symbols in Profusion

Someone once said: "if you wish to taste real Joy and find the way of Truth, choose a profound symbol which pleases you, decorate your room according to your own taste, shut yourself in and meditate".

The symbol is thus a carrier of messages. It is something unknown yet living.

A symbol is alive when someone finds in it a vibrant resonance. Modern symbols have their function at the moment of need and are capable of bringing vibration to a group, a society, an epoch. We have only to remember the swastika.

Hieroglyphic texts and Pharaonic sculptures are rich in symbolism and we wish we could penetrate beyond the mask. The symbol can be inscribed or engraved, but it can not be pronounced. It is the symbol which speaks, and our tendency to want to explain will create a complete barrier to our perceptive listening to this reality.

The Ka often reproduced on tomb walls in the form of two raised arms represents, according to certain interpretations, the double of man, a projection of the Spirit. Its vibrations measure 13,500 units and touch the etheric body; it is the acceptance of a total Presence, a form of splitting in two as a permanent prayer. Some still appreciate the Spirit too much as an abstraction, separated from the body.

In a cosmo-telluric approach the symbol expresses the relation between Earth and Heaven. This is a bipolarity which functions as mediator. Each power point is a possible springboard for ascending to a new level of perception.

In contrast, the Ankh symbolizes the key to Life and holds itself within the material-world limits of 9000 units. Its form is that of the cross whose arms flare toward their extremities and the top is looped liked a hood, the perfect allegory of what has neither beginning nor end but essentially successive reincarnations. This key to life in the hand of a divinity or an initiate indicates that the bearer possesses the universal knowledge and that he knows which sources to draw upon. When this key is placed on the forehead of the initiate, he knows the mysteries but is pledged to secrecy.

These hooded crosses are engraved on entire walls; they are encompassed in Pharaonic texts rich in examples of litanies which play a magic role by their repetition, as would a mantra. This key to life plays a considerable role in Egyptian iconography. Everything relates to life on Earth and to life after life. According to certain contemporary literature we are led to believe that it is the modern world which has discovered this novelty.

Let us return to our Pharaohs on whose foreheads one sees the famous Ureus. The most powerful of these cobras is found on the forehead of Tutankhamen where, at the level of Ureus's eyes, we measure a maximum of 8000 units

Ureus, the cobra on the Pharaoh's forehead. Maximum vibrations are found in three dimensions.

on the physical scale together with 13,500 units on the etheric scale. But the third dimension also makes itself felt at the level of what one could call initiation, with 18,000 units, in such a way as to suggest that a high level of spirituality must dwell there.

These latter vibrations, remaining impregnated with unknown characteristics, are not bound by time. Could they be particles of indestructible cosmic memory which have the faculty of entering into resonance with our centres of consciousness, our chakras?

Ureus symbolizes the vital fluid, but he is also capable of spitting death – the double aspect of an omnipotent inspiration. Sacred texts say that the cobra, carrier of fire, confers power to man when placed in his hand. It is comparable to the fiery fluid of the Hindu kundalini. These emissions at the level of a Pharaoh's forehead are comparable to the beams of light spurting from the eyes of certain personnages depicted in authentic ikons. In both cases the biometer registers the known maximum of 18,000 units.

Some precious masterpieces of Ancient Egypt have undergone numerous mutilations as a result of religious intolerance. But are not the most serious collective crimes always perpetrated in the name of faith?

9. Silent Projection

What should we think of certain statues which can either bring you strength or drain it away from you? Anyone can develop that affinity with things and even with people. Such a level of harmony is difficult to express; it is a little like the difficulty of explaining in words the effects of music. However, the connection with everything living can be perceived after the manner of a blind man who cannot see the sunlight but can feel its warmth.

Let us refer back to the double temple of Kawn Umbu in Upper Egypt. In these sacred precincts the play of polarity is demonstrated by two sculptures, of which there remain unfortunately only a few fragments. This does not affect in any way the possibilities of measuring, so long as these slabs have been left in their original position. On one side there is Horus charged up to 12,000 vibratory units. This is the positive side, the active element, Yang, Heaven.

On the other side there is Sebek the crocodile, the negative, the crawling Yin, underwater or underground, where the measurements fall brutally to 1000 units.

Horus the positive has a concentration of several H rays under his centre and takes on the character of a menhir which emits an energy, permitting man to recharge himself even in a few minutes. In contrast, Sebek the negative has H rays spread out in the four directions, and this is found in the form of the dolmen. The person suffering from stress will do well to choose the latter when he needs to discharge, to

Horus: Yang, charged to 12,000 units, corresponding to a menhir. Hartmann rays concentrated in its centre.

let off steam. But in both cases, and simply to re-establish one's equilibrium, one must comprehend his need for complementary or contradictory interaction.

With many statues this same contact can be felt as a physical support and a link with a force thousands of years old and still present today.

In front of the statue of Sekhmet, known for its terrible vengeance, should one be astonished that the local people are very afraid of it? Of course not. We have already said that its vibration is one of the lowest, only 1000 units. It is interesting to note that persons suffering from anxiety so often make, in passing before it, a sign of shrinking away.

There are vibrations and vibrations, and it is a problem not to confuse a purely technical display with a perception derived from the esoteric domain, especially when it is possible to prove, as we will see farther on, the power of the

Sebek: Yin, charged to 1000 units, corresponding to a dolmen. The H rays are spread out.

imagination. Take for example the two giants, both 20 metres (66 feet) high, which dominate the important cemetery of Thebes dating back to the time of Memnon, about 1400 B.C. For the record, the upper half of one of these giants has crumbled, probably due to an earthquake, yet at sunrise harmonious sounds escape from the section left in place. It is suggested that Memnon is greeting his mother, and one begins to imagine omens in the abundance of either sound or silence.

This is in fact only a technical phenomenon: under the effect of the morning dew and the first rays of sun, doubtless together with a light breeze, the unequal surface of the break emitted sounds, more or less accentuated resonant vibrations. The effect stopped and the statue fell silent once the broken surface had been plastered over.

In old papyrus scrolls there is often talk of healing pillars. These were supposed to have the power to exorcise the evil spirits; a great curative power was attributed to them. A hieroglyphic inscription was carved on the reverse side of the pillar, and to be healed, you had to pour water over these texts. The water became impregnated with magic power and, thus blessed, it was caught in a basin and used on the patient.

In front of a statue some people can be seized with a desire to sense its healing emanations, yet in the beginning they feel no particular sensation. It seems that on Pharaonic sites there does exist a state of grace which favours at once a higher resonance with what was, what is, and what will be.

Thus it can be that suddenly, on a given spot and before a presence having the form of a statue, a silent agreement is born, a mute conformity, a common vibration which will cause matter to seem alive to someone who looks at it. How can this effusion be so powerful after thousands of years?

And so at Luxor, before one of the great stone priests in the sacred enclosure, a statue about 10 metres high (33 feet), we found that life-balance encompassing the three levels of maximum vibrations, that is to say:
– the robustly physical, at 8000 units
– a luminous ethereality of 13,500 units, and
– a serene spiritual presence of 18,000 units,
in spite of the fact that the head of the statue was mutilated. An indescribable reflection of omnipresence and omniscience exists there, whether it is the material statue or pure spirit.

The most beautiful colours are also omnipresent in the

universe, but according to its laws a rainbow only vibrates under certain conditions. . . .

10. Pharaonic Medicine: How much do you know?

How much did you already know at the time when theology, astronomy and medicine were a single science?

Old pieces of bread that were blessed yet perfectly mouldy were carefully conserved in the Coptic convents of Egypt, so as to be used for curing the brothers who fell ill. Such penicillin had been blessed, however.

There was also the physician's manual which told at what moment to administer which plant-based remedy. These were gathered at times precisely determined by astrology. Those doctors knew how to observe a chronobiological rhythm; and we know well that we also are subject to daily, monthly, human, solar, and lunar cycles. Periods of ten days, making three per month, are cited in the texts in the pyramids. Our own chronobiology is still in its infancy, although some attempts have been made in America to try to make an exact science of it.

In the vibratory domain, and especially in the matter of subtle vibrations, the Ancient Egyptians still have a head-start on our trial and error methods. Within the framework of our research it has been possible to reconstitute what we are going to call an Egyptian wave captor, composed simply of copper wire according to a well worked-out plan. It is fascinating to be able to use it for receiving these waves forgotten for centuries. The viewpoint indicator of this receiver corresponds a little with the enormous sculpted zodiac on the ceiling of the upper gallery of the temple of Hathor at Dandarah. Experiments made with the device have demonstrated, for example, that the orientation of a wave coming from the east, a 90-degree wave which we have called the Wave of Ra, the rising sun, gives a vital energy when applied to the human body.

The wave found at 77 degrees, the Wave of Isis, can heal today's malignant tumors. Applied research proves that this is not a casual claim. The multiplication of unhealthy cells is stopped by this method, and we can ask the following question: might we not take this instrument for a perfect cellular equilibrator, being close to a frequency of 27 megahertz, that of the healthy cell? We may also cite the Wave of Ptah located at 65 degrees: this one has a psychological effect and was invoked in Ancient Egypt to prevent foolish mistakes.

The Wave of Osiris is located at "five minutes before midnight" and helps calm the dying, similar to an energy-consciousness expressed in the Ka as an etheric double for the body. Today we treat the dying person as a simple object of the visible world.

The art of mummifying a body forces our admiration. The famous wrappings followed the course of the vital fluid and became a kind of garment of light. The embalmers knew only too well how to maintain the etheric body, so well that at the museum of Cairo the mummies have been declared to be still living. The cry of distress they utter when disturbed in their eternal sleep has caused the administration to put them in a place sheltered from the curious.

Recipes for aromatic compounds used in different magical operations have been noted down in the temples of Edfu and Philae. Bizarre processes are found in ancient documents, such as the crushed bones of frogs and the claws of bats, but these do not inspire our contemporary pharmaceutical companies. In many remedies intended as sedatives one finds mixtures of oil and honey.

We can only marvel before their surgical methods. We must admire the perfect suturing of large wounds and the use of splints and plaster for fractures, just as today.

Beyond a certain level of superstition, medicine was really an art and a science. We learn there were already specialists, such as eye doctors, and dentists, 3000 years before Jesus Christ. The specialist in internal medicine was called "he who knows all about internal fluids".

The Ancient Egyptians reveal a very broad knowledge of mathematics and astronomy.

How long it is, how long it is, the road toward the True Knowledge of Man.

CHAPTER 4

India

1. Backdrop

India, "this land of meditation", presents multiple faces to Europeans. If you think you'll find Illumination at the next corner, it turns out to be a meeting with Misery.

For the Hindu, however, suffering and poverty in this world are quite relative. He does not feel the tragedy of his conditions in the same way as we do; the masses live in a quiet state, in an inertia from which they do not appear to want to escape.

But this slowness is without doubt indispensable if India wishes to remain India, without becoming a bad copy of a western country.

There are also the days of celebration and then we see the side that is Dream, where the tales of a thousand and one nights really come to life. Leaving their marble palaces, the princesses wear their silken saris in shimmering colours – what a beautiful air of nobility in the bearing of these goddesses. Tomorrow they must earn their less colourful living alongside those beautiful, sweet-faced, dirty children, whose wide eyes reflect the deep movement of their souls.

One is charmed by the light and the lucidity of India's old intellectuals: the individual human is not the centre of the Universe. Like the other creatures, he has only an assigned place in the cosmic order.

Through our broad geobiological investigation we will open a small skylight into this part of the Orient, in pursuit of one or another power point but without singing the praises of any hypothetical Katmandus.

The Indian or the Hindu knows better than we how to live in harmony with nature. His affinity with the land is

Termite mound and architecture of Hindu temple: H rays concentrated under the cone or the centre.

spontaneous and innate; he embraces the earth. Through contact with the element earth he knows how to take in that radiation and, according to his sensitivity, knows how to influence his energy system. Like most of the nomads, the Oriental stores the earth's impulses through the soles of his feet.

Within the framework of these fields of influence, of permanent creativity, the search for equilibrium is focused on the structure which should at least preserve but also condense and amplify the power of the location.

Here we must choose among innumerable temples, some of which have retained strategic fragments of the original architecture. Among the various religions, the focal points of the holy places in India are found particularly in the following locations:

- in Buddhist temples: in front of the Buddha;
- in mosques: in front of the East recess;
- in Jain temples: in the centre as in the temples of Shiva;
- in the temples of Shiva: directly under the cone of the edifice, at the fountain situated in a perpendicular line from the centre of the cone where, of course, the sacred water serves for absolution in a ritual of purification.

Complementing the above, we should add that in the Russian churches, as in the Coptic churches of Egypt, the force focus is found in the centre of the interior square.

And in our ancient Christian cathedrals it is found, most often, in the centre of the chancel or of the dome.

In all these places the passage of underground water, a living element without form, maintains a permanent influence on our energy system.

This power point is vertical music for the Hindu initiate, causing his centres of conscience to vibrate – sculpting a noble silence.

2. The Perplexed Christian

Let us go back to our modest measurements and our little lamp.

All the sanctuaries in India have in common the fact that the Hartmann network is absent from the centre and, as at

Hindu temple architecture echoing the termite mound.

Chartres or in Egypt, a spray of compacted lines is found pushed back from the exterior of the structure in all four directions.

We must admit that in this domain, and in relation to the Occident, India provides surprising confirmations.

To simplify our work we will isolate two principal currents from the multiple avenues offered in India:

1. the Moslem tendency = the mosques;
2. the temples of Shiva, called the supreme creative force, indeterminate in time, selected among innumerable divinities.

And what do we find?

The values in units are much superior to those in our Christian churches!

Taking as our point of comparison the cathedral of Chartres, with 11,000 units, we discover — in a manner that can be reproduced — that the mosque, regardless of where it is situated geographically, gives a reading of 12,000 . . .

Our astonishment is unbounded in the old Hindu temples of Shiva where there are always 14,000 units!

Only on these latter places of high vibrations can the physical body succeed to another state of being on the metaphysical path.

In the wake of these comparative measurements we have to pose a disconcerting question: what is the significance of these higher values, why do these Moslem and Hindu places of worship have a higher level of vibrations than our Christian structures? Is this not a slap in the face to our rather arrogant Christian conception, perhaps imagining ourselves alone to be the favoured children, even at a higher level?

Even so, we would like to be able to explain why it is that we always find the same values, regardless of the category of the place of worship. Why are there always 12,000 units in the mosques and 14,000 units in the temples of Shiva, with this prevailing independently of the geographical position?

One could advance the hypothesis that, within the structure of an identical religious concept, there could be a system of resonance. We should not forget that our entire universe is built according to systems of resonance or vibrational harmonies. So as to try to illustrate this phenomenon, let us recall by analogy this well-known little experimental game:

Two violins are tuned, one of them is placed on a table and with the other violin someone begins to play a single note. The attentive observer will remark that the same string being plucked on one violin will begin to vibrate on the other. These examples of "sympathetic" harmony or resonance can be multiplied.

Has not each religion – whether Buddhism, Islam or Christianity – adopted its own vibrational form in order to arouse in a specific way, within the finished edifice, the centres of consciousness adapted to its own way of faith?

We must once again emphasize the repeated presence of an underground watercourse in these focal points. It appears more and more evident that this fluid, moving substance guarantees an essential basic vibration and becomes an indispensable permanent support. Indian mythology depicts the watercourse by the serpent, the Naga or Naja with seven heads, which expresses infinite fecondity.

We will benefit, however, by making a distinction between constructions dating from ancient times and the more recent temples. Such knowledge is found only in the old sanctuaries as well as in our cathedrals built from the eleventh to the thirteenth century. The builders who followed took into account neither the site nor the wave form, and these new places of worship have lost the basic vibration (if they ever had it). Of course, we can say that a spiritual effect can be created anywhere, but these edifices were conceived for the multitudes. The influences stemming from the site and the synchronization of forms obviously had their *raison d'être*.

A concrete example found in India illustrates the difference between a temple having ancient characteristics and the most modern one of New Delhi, the Laksmi Narain which was financed in 1938 by a family of rich Buddhists. There, between some statues of Shiva with a fixed and distant gaze, we are no more touched than if we had gone into the hubbub of a department store. The vibrations of Laksmi Narain are maintained over its entire surface at 6500 units, according to the Bovis scale, and, as for the Hartmann telluric network, it sings everywhere in a perfectly regular fashion, as if there were nothing at all unusual.

And this same dullness and this same vibratory poverty in the midst of luxury are found wherever the places of adoration are dedicated to the gods of money.

3. A Vibration which creates a Change

In India, on the sites where we register a vibration of 14,000 units, we find people who are extraordinary to our eyes. We would like to know their secret: how do they know how to draw benefit from these cosmo-telluric forces and even feed on them?

Little by little we cross a new threshold of subtle vibrations. It is remarkable to note that the spots which give us a special vitality are, as always in India, in relation with a quite special corner of the land which has been known as a holy place since time immemorial. It is the home of a "Spirit of the Earth", a place of contact with creative genius. Cosmo-telluric exchanges are without any doubt more intense there; the higher and more rapid vibrations are capable even of transforming the human physique.

These exceptional men and women living such a mutation in these places already have no more need of earthly nourishment. But they know how to draw their energy from this vibratory universe, which we really have trouble understanding and accepting. You have to have seen it, to have verified it, without illusion, without imagination, in order to accept that there really are enigmas under the sun.

Across the vast dry regions of the Indian peninsula there are small corners to be found where it seems that the Spirit breathes more strongly than elsewhere. And when a visitor has the chance to impregnate himself in it, it can happen that a more familiar sense of the divine subsequently develops in him.

One of the most striking encounters we experienced merits to be mentioned here, although these surprising super-beings generally seem neither astonishing nor disturbing to anyone of the neighborhood. Satimatha, which in Hindu means "holy mother", is a robust women of 80 years living in a small ashram in the desert, about 60 kilometres (36 miles) from Jodhpur. What appears unbelievable is that she has taken no nourishment for 35 years. Is it possible to be in perfect health without eating or drinking? Our doctors deny this categorically, yet there is

In Indian mythology the seven-headed serpent represents the watercourse and expresses fecundity.

sufficient proof to show that it is not a mystification of some kind. We are face to face with a person who is capable of nourishing herself from Prana and from cosmo-telluric energy! Exclusively? No, she blesses the visitors and the fruits and vegetables which they bring her in abundance and which are then given to the inhabitants of the ashram. Might that not be a subtle bit of shrewdness: the products of the earth and the people who surround her also create a reservoir of energies!

Nevertheless, it is certain that the Prana is her vitamin from the air, what others might try to explain by electrons, ether, negative ions or tachyons, or electromagnetic fields.

What a temptation to be able to learn to live like Satimatha! Yet it is not useless to make one mini-effort without pretentions: the luminous energy-nutrition which the attentive observer can capture from the edges of sunlit tree leaves, silhouetted against the blue of the sky, or the length of palm branch deploying its pointed antennae in all directions. Let us see if those captured vibrations might not succeed in giving us the impression of having been fed, at least for a brief period of time. The result of the exercise cannot be known quickly, especially since our bodies have been conditioned and our training can only be a personal condition; the aroma of dinner can demolish everything, we come down to earth, to bread for the body and wine for the blood.

Satimatha has something else to intrigue us: when someone comes from another village, seeking her to go and cure a sick man or a sick cow, she goes there with such speed that no one can keep up with her. Her pace is then a kind of slipping over the miles as if on skates, but slightly above the ground, without touching the earth. This seems improbable to us, and yet it is reality. After all, did not Christ himself know this energy from the void, knowing how to use this cushion of air for walking across the waters? Or did he also know how to use the highest form of cosmic energy, a transfer of power drawn from empty space?

This conception of empty space containing a very powerful energy was already demonstrated by Wilhelm Reich more than half a century ago. It seems that, for the moment at least, only the Orientals – and among them only those who have acquired a Knowledge – are capable of applying this *tour de force* in using these energies discharged from the reservoirs of the void.

Within the framework of our investigations, and so as to understand better the exceptional qualities of this prestigious Satimatha, we must at any price be able to measure the intensity of vibrations of the precise spot she occupies for meditating and sleeping. We had scarcely thought to formulate our timid request for authorization to penetrate her privacy before she gave us an affirmative answer – even before we had uttered a single word.

And there, on the spots she had chosen, where she recharged herself in order to establish this famous earth–cosmos contact, we discovered once again the highest vibration of the temple of Shiva, 14,000 units. So we find ourselves back on the same track.

When our hands brushed hers involuntarily, we felt a shock. It was very troubling to note that this contact was not the touch of a real, physical human hand, yet there she was before our eyes in flesh and blood. This touch felt like a gentle burn, a dematerialized contact giving the impression of plunging into a thick layer of spider webs.

How we would have liked to know more about this curious phenomenon of the conscious mutation of the physical body!

Is it permissible to admit that by our unpremeditated gesture it was possible to touch the thick etheric body of Satimatha, still in mutation? Certain photographic exposures of the Kirlian type confirm that at the instant of the death of the physical body, the "pattern", the bioplasma or, if you prefer, the lines of the etheric currents, are enormously intensified. Is this a phase of high tension within a process which goes slowly, but which becomes a real short-circuit in the case of a violent death?

Satimatha is a living example who approaches the experience of conscious mutation of the body accomplished by the "Mother", the companion of Sri Aurobindo at Pondicherry in the south of India.

For this inner work of mutation, and to be able to enter into relation with a particular vibration, is it indispensable to choose a given place? Without doubt. These extraordinary people living in parallel with two bodies need a permanent vibratory underpinning. This metaphysical stimulant is provided for Satimatha by her disciples who murmur day and night, without interruption: Ram-Ram-Ram. . .

Ram contains the cycle of the sun, of the fire (the inner fire), of the moon. So long as the rotation goes on, life continues.

The elements of life without nourishment are, in this case, a kind of cumulation of the vibration of the word endlessly repeated, the intense cosmo-telluric influence of the spot, and the energies of the fruits and vegetables presented. But look out! How surprised we were, we four visitors, that after leaving her we fell into a deep, exhausted sleep for several hours in broad daylight.

Does she know how to appropriate the vitality of her guests? This is not impossible, for on a smaller scale and often without knowing it, we often draw on the energy of others, like little vampires.

4. Earth – Man – Chakras

In Sanskrit the word chakra means "wheel" – the wheel of life, the vitality of the wheel which keeps our wagon rolling.

Without getting into all the ins and outs of the living energy spiral which nourishes our energy centres, let us simply declare that India remains the cradle of an appealing Teaching which knows how to transform an earthly energy into other more subtle energies and how to prepare man to receive them.

A person standing with his chakras aligned vertically, from the base of the torso to the top of the head, should be linked to the Cosmos. Seated on the ground he will have a more physical and material contact with terrestrial energy and Nature. This interpenetration will fortify the energy centre which the Japanese call "Hara", located a few centimetres below the umbilicus. In order to condition himself to support pain, the Nipponese disciple will give himself vigorous blows with the fist – which is not recommended for fragile Occidentals!

Nowadays we divide the chakras into three zones: pelvis, solar plexus, and head. Each zone contains three centres of consciousness, making nine in all. The conception of seven chakras was perfectly valid until the nineteenth and twentieth centuries. It was in harmony with the known existence of seven planets. With the discovery of two additional planets we have entered into a new evolutionary cycle, and a new analogical relation has become established between the universe and man.

With the discovery of Neptune in 1848 and Pluto in 1936, the evolving human must deal with this process and adapt himself to it. Oh how slowly it goes! While the schools of yoga and the abundant literature of psi in the West continue to repeat and to plagiarize the theory of 7, the burgeoning recycling to 9 chakras is taking its time.

In India the Earth is respectfully thought of as a living being animated by a spiritual current. Man is not cut off from the contemplative life, and he feels the characteristic pulsation of a place as if his human cells had preserved that coded cosmic memory linking them by natural affinity to a vibrational All. Everyone has been able at one time or another to observe that, in order to let a natural energy flow through one's self, it is enough to pick out a healthy tree, a peak, a spring or a rock – and it will be better still if the site selected is neutral within the Hartmann network.

Even rock is not dead matter. It may be that it does not have conscious particles but, just like us, it is subject to a determinable life cycle. It has its youth, its old age. It will die. Each life form has its own clock.

It seems that everything is programmed to reach its end. Is it not stupefying when, at a given moment, an important discovery is made here and yet, at nearly the same time, it is also made at the other end of the world? You can always say that espionage was possible, but there are simultaneous revelations in certain brains without there having been any communication between them. If there is a superior Intelligence pulling the strings behind the scenes of this world, it is to be hoped that it is aiming at a better intelligence in our societies.

So, beyond all geopolitical considerations, our continents are evolving more and more into zones of new energies. The spiritual evolution is pouring itself into the laboratories of the intelligentsia and creating the new symbols of the electronic era. The current of a Knowledge thousands of years old, which has invaded the Occident from the Orient, is spreading out, enlivened and often enriched thanks to the help of computer processing. Meetings and forums for a transcendental opening in science are being held on all sides. They are going to bring, happily, a stimulating spark right into the parlours of distinguished lassitude.

This is a good place to stop and take a look at the well-filled safe holding the files on man–earth–chakras–cosmos.

5. *Strange Vibrations of Love*

In India it is not unusual to meet, just outside or inside a temple, a being of light who, anonymously, makes you a gift of a flow of compassion-affection, of an emission of soothing waves. During our discreet taking of measurements the temple officials who are watching understand intuitively what is happening between our method and these holy places. Their wide dark eyes even reflect a blessing in our direction. We splash about in the holy water and an abundance of flowers, without shoes, feeling the cold floor beneath our feet.

This permanence of love vibrations and human warmth is part of India's fascination. It is even found in the preparation of a festive meal, where as an invited Westerner one might fear that the food would be poorly tolerated. But not at all. You will have been told previously that everything will go very well, for we are told "this food is prepared with strong vibrations of love"!

There is something to leave us perplexed, but have we not often laughed at the old sayings which taught us that the good or bad humour of the cook would permeate the meal he had prepared?

And are we not closer than we might have thought to that definition of the vibration of love uttered by Teilhard de Chardin, that it could be the strongest of energies, the greatest of the activating forces? Man is only beginning, and timidly at that, to have a glimpse of the value of love.

Thus the most perfect form of love in existence would show itself in a permanent fusion with the higher Presence, the *unio mystica*.

The poet who knows how to translate and to bring back to the human level the attractive vibrations of love may be

the one who inspires this delicate incantation of newlyweds
during their ceremony around the sacred fire:

"I am masculine
You are feminine
I am heaven
You are earth
together we are the universe . . ."

CHAPTER 5

Tibetan Monasteries

1. Buddhist Power Points at High Altitude

It is into a valley of the Indus, on one of the highest of the Himalayan plateaux and where Tibetan Buddhism still survives in a hundred monasteries, that we are going to compare our measurements with those made in the holy places of the low-lying lands. The entire Indo-Tibetan plateau is one large power point. Its configuration threw the Hartmann network out of its habitual pattern, for here the links are stretched out and irregular. Was this caused by the powerful tectonic shock provoked by continental drift, or is it due to a specific arrangement of votive monuments which work astutely to spread out the telluric lines in populated areas?

It will be under towering summits, culminating at more than 7000 metres (23,000 feet) that we breathlessly climb the raised steps to these sanctuaries, which also contain unique treasures of religious art. We will remain at altitudes between 2500 and 4000 metres (8000–13,000 feet). How marvellous to find in this immense desert of rocks an oasis where, even at 3700 metres (12,000 feet), tasty little apricots ripen! These are dried and constitute a precious reserve for the winter.

So, nearer to heaven yet with feet still on the ground, we are going to concentrate on that farthest corner of Northwest India, the sparsely populated Ladakh with ten inhabitants to the square mile. This region plunges like a finger into a geopolitical wound between China, Tibet, the USSR, and Kashmir. Today attached to India, its strategic importance is made obvious by the permanent parade of military trucks which cross, like dusty cockroaches, the high passes and narrow roads from rich Kashmir during the four months of summer.

These high plateaus of the Himalayan chains will be isolated from the rest of the world during eight months of winter.

Here the house, the dwelling takes on more importance. In

winter the ground floor is abandoned to the animals and the life of the family takes refuge on the second floor. Because there are important temperature variations between night and day, the kitchen is the only heated room and it is here that the people sleep. Outside the thermometer can push down as far as minus 35 degrees Centigrade (minus 31 degrees Fahrenheit).

What especially interests us in our research is the geobiological profile of these monasteries, whose builders were not ignorant of divining (which today we called geobiology). They knew how to adapt a discerning architecture to proportions which fit well on the sites . . . and to the telluric networks.

In this desert propitious for revelations, nevertheless favouring fertile imaginations and the proliferation of supernatural beings, Buddha's smile remains imperturbable and his gaze remains both interior and distant.

Water, rare in these regions, is used for Tibetan rites of initiation; it confirms the vow and the promise of the candidate. The gesture of this vow is the hand which touches the earth and takes it as witness. The vibrational strength of this exchange corresponds to that of a balanced physique, which is 8000 units.

Buddha's hand, opening before you with palm toward the heavens and offering itself as a gift, immediately produces 14,000 units.

What should no longer be surprising is that all the interiors of the monasteries are located in a vast neutral zone, in relation to the H network. A marvellous calm reigns at the level of the prayer benches, slightly elevated from the floor and covered with carpets. In contrast, wherever there is a spot intended to radiate more intensely, as before a large Buddha, the powerful telluric point is composed of a mass of six north-south rays and nine east-west rays.

In every one of these monasteries there are four timber columns of Himalayan cedar grouped at the centre, and each one of these places will give a vibration of 14,000 units. However, we are not in a Hindu temple, which would have the same characteristic of 14,000 vibrations, and we were expecting to find a different value. Given the identical vibrations in these Buddhist sites, we might ask if there is not a close relationship between Buddhism and Hinduism!

There we find the three levels of the universe: the underground world, the earth's surface, and the celestial world. Whether with the column or with the cross, we have our symbols of the union of earth and heaven, of intimacy with the divine.

These symbols of union linking the low with the high become power, and they correspond to the spinal column of the human body, the vertical support.

The temple column is not located haphazardly in just any place, but it is oriented in such a way that, ingeniously, its shadow passes over the threshold at specific times of the Tibetan calendar. This calendar dates back to the birth of Buddha 2500 years ago. The Pole Star was supposed to be the summit of the sacred column.

The dome is positioned on these four pillars; it is square at the base. This brings us back to Chinese symbolism which has the heaven covering and the earth supporting, but there is also the conception that heaven is round and the earth square, within its solid, material limits. The union of square and circle is found again in the orchestration of two levels: architectural and ritual.

Tibetan Buddhism, always in concrete dialogue with the existing telluric current, represented by the serpent, holds that the rainbow is a celestial serpent. The Asians believe that he breathes or drinks river water. The rainbow is without doubt the most colourful of the relationships between heaven and earth, a two-way communications bridge, expressing the cosmo-terrestrial exchange in all regions.

If for Noah of the Old Testament the rainbow was a sign of the covenant, for the Tibetan it is the seven-coloured stairway by which Buddha comes down again from heaven: it appears but remains elusive. It is a place of passage linked to cyclical renewal. When we have the privilege of being bathed for an instant in the intense light of a rainbow, a strong vibration of 13,500 units shows us that it is possible to orchestrate the colours of life.

Some information for those who would like to discover for themselves, on the spot, the effect of the powerful vibrations of 14,000 units inside the monasteries of Ladakh: you will find them in the temples of Phyang, Hemis, Alchi, Stakna, Spituk, Thikse and Likir. At Stok this vibration is found only in the meditation chamber of the royal palace.

At Mulbeck this high vibration is found before the enormous statue of Maitreya, in front of and at the level of his feet. The entrance courtyard is well guarded by the usual 18 Hartmann rays, which have already made themselves known at the pyramids. However, this was the only barrier of its kind encountered in the whole country, and it coincides with the boundary of a geographical zone where the impressive line of Tibetan monasteries begins. There is a small temple beside the statue of Mulbeck, a good omen for our penetration of Tibetan geobiology: it is oriented exactly north-south, and the dimensions between the four central pillars of wood are, to our surprise, those of the H network, being 2 metres north-south and 2.5 metres east-west. Why is it that we find exactly those measurements?

In the temple of Lakham Soma at Alchi, in front of the great Buddha, we find six H rays concentrated north-south and nine rays east-west. This is the plan that we will find on all the Tibetan religious sites where there is one especially strong and condensed point; it radiates on the neutral spots intended for prayer and meditation. It is said that the four Tibetan temples of Alchi are the best preserved of all. They are at an altitude of 3100 metres (10,170 feet) and the site offers high radioactivity. There are a thousand and one miniature Buddhas painted with great finesse on the walls, of which a part are unfortunately a little too faded. These are doubtless mantras in pictorial form.

The temple at Likir was the first Buddhist monastery constructed in Ladakh. According to legend the site is enircled by two large royal Nagas – water spirits – meaning our terrestrial currents. There is a very active life in this monastery. On the day of our visit we can only marvel at the birth of a masterpiece, intended for the celebrated holy festival of Likir. This is the creation of a mandala by four monk-artists who, seated on the ground, trickle tiny coloured stones along previously traced lines. They identify fully with their work – these monks, before starting to work, have prepared themselves through several days of meditation. To think that this work of art will be destroyed after the ceremony . . . this is their philosophy, in harmony with the organization of a universe where everything submits to the law of impermanence.

There is a line of monks meditating near a wall in a small lateral chapel, always in the neutral zone and free of H rays.

They are submitted to particularly rigorous rules. We are astonished that on this spot nothing registers at the level of physical vibration, but the biometer shows that there is direct contact with a vibration of 14,000 units joined to the etheric body.

Nothing shows on the low side of the third sector of the spiritual domain, nor is there anything on the high end.

Even if they attach no importance to the physical, the place is going to compensate for that supply of energy. The site is not banal, because a Hartmann ray passes all along the seats. This expedient provides a subtle way of being able to concentrate on a specific aspect while neglecting the others. One must admit that only an enlightened diviner could play this refined game.

It seems that at Likir the builders took into account the presence of Nagas, those subterranean streams, and of the earth's impulse. The hundred monks living in this place are nearly spoiled children: everything coincides so that the emphasis is put on developing their etheric bodies, and they can hold themselves in the assigned level of their spiritual development without a false note and truly "between two waters".

A secret elite

We keep on hoping, almost feverishly, that we will find holy places where there would be an even higher vibration of 18,000 units such as ought to be present at every power point. Without these peak points of force we will be condemned to make superficial deductions, classifying these places at the level of 14,000 units everywhere. This corresponds to rituals, to meditation, to the search for liberation from earthly suffering or from ignorance.

These precise points of high vibration at 18,000 were finally found in two monasteries: Likir, the oldest, dating back to 1065, and Rizong, the most recent, built in 1840. There a spiritual guidance inhabits a power point, permitting the High Lama to attain the state of Buddha, to bring into focus the virtues of wisdom and compassion.

The third site is a hidden jewel, an abandoned corner of a primitive temple adjoining the monastery of Spituk to the southwest of Leh at an altitude of 3600 metres (11,800) feet. It affords an extensive view over the Indus and tributary valleys.

Tibetan Monasteries

This abandoned holy place, on a base of hard-packed earth with raw logs for columns, lies beyond the magnificently sculpted windows of the large monastery. The total lack of ornamentation, the particularly calm atmosphere together produce a serene mood. This state of well-being is confirmed with the biometer where we obtain a maximum of vibrations balanced for the physical as well as the energetic body. Finally, the authentic power point is found with vibrations of 18,000, but it seems to have been abandoned or ignored.

In the renovated principal monastery of Spituk we enter another world; masks and destructive monsters are crammed in there. Beneath the god Shug-Den there are, curiously, only 3000 vibrations, which finds expression in uneasiness and flight. Nearby, under a crushing pile of effigies of divinities, there must be some interferences causing oppression and agitation. The biometer always showed us low vibrations in that mass.

However down below on the packed earth, at a distance, there is a very valuable cosmo-telluric radiation. The monks of the monastery go down there to seek at a distance what they already have close at hand.

These three chosen holy places have the same characteristics; the same conditions are brought together in such a way that their selection could certainly not have come about by chance.

Rizong, Likir and Spituk are situated geologically in the granitic zone north of the Indus. The layers of granite which are the foundations of these monasteries are tilted to the vertical, and this could contribute to their rate of radioactivity, which is higher than 26 microroentgens per hour each. These three Tibetan power points have an intensity of gamma radioactivity nearly triple that at Kashmir, and it is often felt even by those who are not accustomed to it.

According to the biometer the energetic intensity on this Himalayan granite is 10,000 units, about 10 per cent stronger than on the red granite of Upper Egypt. Doubtless the verticality of the strata plays a complementary rôle.

These three monasteries knew how to orchestrate the harmony of bipolarity in orienting their buildings within the terrestrial magnetic field, exactly north-south in fact. Thus these three power points have one of the highest vibration rates, resting on four specifications: orientation, strong radio-

75

Power point of Buddhist meditation.

activity, vertical granite strata, and an absence of all disturbing
telluric rays in their interiors.

These Himalayan focal points truly reflect their landscape of
steep summits and smiling oases. Contrasts and emotions are
the grand scenery of this Tibetan Buddhism, whose doctrine
is detachment from all things. Perhaps they arrive at their goal
between the zenith of the blue vault and the nadir which
makes them creep through its dark subterranean world.

In thinking about the main doors of these temples, one
seeks vainly some allegories, opposing positive to negative,
such as we have in our Christian sanctuaries. Buddhism does
not want to present the negative; the doorway to Nirvana is
attractive. The Masters coming on wings of Compassion
have their sincere disciples under all latitudes. Then there are

the cunning who extol this detachment from all things and who know how to incite their followers to abandon all their goods with joy. It is not useless to be reminded on a threshold that positive and negative go together, for in these cases one must keep one's eyes open.

2. The Great Himalayan Suture

In this chaotic mixture of colourful rocks, lying between the south slope of the Himalayas and the enormous granite mass stretching north of the Indus, we are in the zone of the Himalayan suture where a high radioactivity is registered. It is a particularly turbulent line of tectonic demarcation, a rock crystallized deep down in the magma mass which, 60 million years ago, formed the Trans-Himalayan mountain chain, one of the longest on our globe.

Remember the grandiose story of continental drift: 220 million years ago, it is said, the subcontinent of India was joined to Africa, Australia and Antarctica – what a giant of a continent that must have been! And then India began to wander toward the north, a hundred-million-year promenade leading up to the Great Collision, beginning about 50 million years ago.

Thus India and Asia grew nearer little by little until, the dense undersea formations forming a barrier, the subcontinent began to slip under its Asian neighbour. The ultimate collision between the two plates caused them to buckle, the joint rising very high under the great pressure. So it becomes understandable why today we find marine deposits in lands a considerable distance from sea level. There are also precious stones, and the activity of old volcanoes has left traces of dark folds, making for splotches of chiaroscuro in an otherwise varied and colourful setting.

One can expect a higher than normal radioactivity all along this zone of collision and faults, and the Geiger-Muller counter was rarely quiet, oscillating continually between 26 and 30 microroentgens per hour although a normal average would be 20. The power points of monasteries are situated on the granite in this zone, and the builders certainly chose their sites in relation to the play of natural forces. In order to avoid creating a graph lacking poetry, let us state that the radioactivity at Srinagar in

Kashmir is only 50 per cent of the normal, that is to say, 10 microroentgens an hour, whether inside dwellings or outside on Lake Dal. But the closer one approaches to the Himalayan suture zone the more the radioactivity increases, and it will triple at Lamayuru at an altitude of 3700 metres (12,000 feet). Simultaneously, the biometer shows an intense terrestrial energy which is independent of the diminishing oxygen. To the east, in the direction of China and where the granite is interspersed with ferruginous rocks, the rust-coloured scenery gives us a reading of 9500 units. The presence of the iron drives the compass crazy and it spins in fanciful directions, not knowing which way to turn.

But what is the terrestrial H network doing with the H in Himalaya, in this environment of intense energies having a special impact on the physical body?

For the first time in the history of our investigations it is a state of total confusion!

The Hartmann network on our globe has been faithfully found up to now with regular dimensions. To be precise: from east to west in Europe, Asia, the Far East, the Americas, and from the Far North to the southern seas.

This great Himalayan fold has upset the rule concerning the rays running east-west, for they are farther apart than the usual 2 metres (6 feet 6 inches) from north to south. In contrast, the lines running north-south are not affected and hold within their usual spacing of 2.5 metres (8 feet 2 inches) from east to west. (See diagram in Chapter Two.) In our country there is often a local geological anomaly when the distances between the Hartmann rays are irregular or disturbed.

The farther one gets from the summit of a mountain the more the distances between the Hartmann rays spread out toward north and south, this space becoming 3.5 to 3.7 metres (11 feet 6 inches to 12 feet), even 4.1 metres (13 feet 6 inches) at times. But as one approaches a summit the spacing between the rays shrinks and we find 2.7, 2.9, and 3.3 metres (8 feet 10 inches, 9 feet 6 inches and 10 feet 8 inches). This troubling and rather special fact could well

Some power points will show, as in front of this Buddha, a condensation of H rays with six running north-south and nine running east-west.

be one of the keys explaining the use of these linear spacings in the construction of dwellings. We will come back to this when studying the astonishing houses.

3. *An Old Stupa*

Sometimes funerary, sometimes religious, this monument has a sanskrit name: stupa. Its outline is found frequently along the roads of the Buddhist landscape.

Its foundation will be square, although for the oldest structures it is circular. It raises its distinctive tower above four square stone plates, which contain the remains or the ashes of an important person. It is crowned with a spire or another pointed form, and the question arises: do these structures have a special influence on the region or the inhabitants?

There is good reason to be disoriented if you try to trust the compass in establishing some benchmarks concerning the positioning of the stupas. There is no relationship either with the terrestrial magnetic field or with the classical north-south alignment or even with the rising or setting sun. Nothing at all. Once again this imported Buddhism is going to show us that these stone symbols have no interest in proving their value. It is up to us to recognize the error, the pretension of our desire to find an order for everything.

Our working hypothesis is that the orientation of a stupa blends in certain cases with the natural form of the valley; entire rows of them will follow the characteristic contour of the cliffs. Sometimes the stupa faces a summit, whose rushing stream at its feet threatens pitilessly to carry it away. For the inhabitants it makes an obvious barrier against destructive spirits, and so you find lines of stupas like sentinels at the entrances of villages and monasteries.

What interests us are the vibration and the impact of the stupa. On all four sides, exactly in the middle of the façade, a force line crosses through the stupa. It seems allowable to

This stupa in the centre of the temple of Sum Tsek at Alchi was originally outside. This temple was built around it later and became its stage setting. The three great deities which surround it reflect the well-known 14,000 units of vibration.

propose that this is an emission deriving from the shape, for our tests of little stupas, reconstituted in small scale, show the presence of these same four lines.

These lines obviously cross in the centre of the structure; the central spire can stimulate an emission of 12,000 units in the four directions.

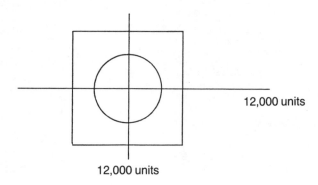

This is surely a votive structure whose power to concentrate energy in its body can radiate beyond the limits of the site. All the same, due to its 12,000 vibrations corresponding in a surprising manner to the muezzin's call from the tower of a mosque, the stupa has the same function of a subtle reminder, a little like our church bells. These latter have however a striking power which will make a quiet village vibrate at 13,000 units, while the vibration of the same bells in the hubbub of a city is reduced to practically nothing.

Coming back to our stupas, the force lines are found without exception in all our on-site measurements. Is this a voluntary and calculated geomancy?

Might not these structures also be tabernacles housing the influence of the famous Naga – hence the underground current? This could also apply to the amplification of a site's influence. Thus it was with real joy that we discovered on a sixteenth-century fresco in the temple of Hemis that the stupa was conceived with foreknowledge of these influences and was not intended to remain dead stone. This fresco confirmed the terrestrial current, symbolized by the snake Naga who is placed on the stupa where a median line enters, as shown on the sketch, and he comes out on one of the sides. We find this play of two movements and two directions on the spot. Pointing upwards, the Naga's head distributes his impulse through the stupa's "antenna". This cosmo-telluric connection in the four directions thus extends to the six dimensions; it is said that the Nagas in cemeteries symbolize the six perfections.

Let us contemplate the stupa with its four rectangular plates ranged atop the foundation, one above the other in tiers, a metaphor for contemporary geobiology. A discreet parallel will be found again in one of the chapters of the Illumination of Buddha, describing the noble truths:

1. the root – the pain;
2. the cause of the pain;
3. the cure for the pain;
4. the path which leads to an end of pain.

If geobiology is seeking the root, the cause, the cure and the way to avoid pain, Buddhist philosophy explains that the cure for earthly pain is to not be reborn!

It is true that we feel so tied to suffering that we do not feel qualified to liberate ourselves. Buddha's smile reflects his victory over suffering. It is not a patronizing attitude but an invitation to the human creature to get away from those trifles to which it attaches too much importance.

Sometimes we find, in the shade of a protective roof, a formation of three little stupas symbolizing
    wisdom, compassion, energy.

The three receptacles represent the soul, the word and the body of Buddha. A piece of wood has been placed inside the first one – a symbol of life?

The stupa remains the symbol of Buddha's omniscience. Like a night-watchman in man's fog of ignorance.

4. *The Astonishing House*

Astonishing at first glance, for it would be the geobiological ideal for a healthy dwelling, without any terrestrial disturbance inside, without any H ray crossings. The Hartmann grids always stop at the corners and the edges of the house. Wherever measurements have been made in independent dwellings, in temples and in their attached residences, there is always the same surprising reading.

What was this Knowledge of the builders, uniting geomancy and the dwelling?

Obvious curiosity motivated our attempt to understand better. We have gathered together bits and scraps of answers to the questions we asked, as follows:

1. Well-being is due principally to the use of natural construction materials, such as packed earth and paving blocks mixed with dried dung. Their polarity has been respected, which is no longer the case with contemporary cut stone.

2. There is no disturbance from terrestrial rays and diagonals; they have been pushed outside the dwelling. The natural spacing of the Hartmann network in this Himalayan region was used to achieve neutral zones in the interior. Inasmuch as the interval of H rays in a dwelling oriented, for example, in the same sense as a stupa could be as much as 4 metres from north to south, they could place their small bedrooms within the "flow of blessings" and thus feel protected.

3. Radioactivity is higher than normal. One can measure 8000 vibratory units, the perfect balance for the physical body, within an interior composed of wooden ceiling beams, bamboo and packed earth.

4. The construction labourers chant while working and placing the building blocks. Is it unthinkable that their movements harmonized with the rhythmic vibrations of their chant could modify the molecular structure of the materials, and that all this is part of their super-science?

5. It is important to choose a propitious site before work commences. The place must not be inhabited by a subterreanean god.

The astonishing house

No terrestrial network perturbs its interior. The geological structure of the Himalayas is unusual and has without doubt been used for construction of the dwelling with full knowledge of the facts.

Sixteenth-century fresco in the temple of Hemis showing the Naga, representing the telluric current influencing the stupa built there.

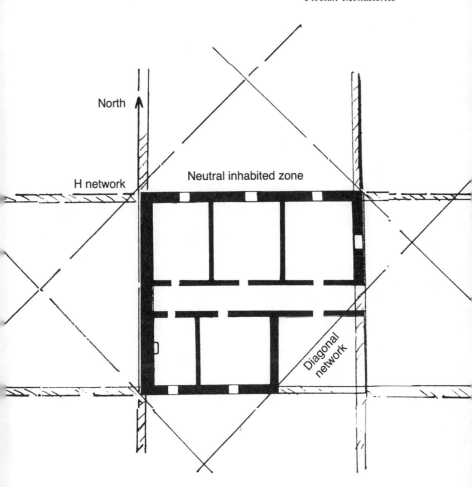

He who determined the place of construction, the *onpo*, was generally an astrologer who confirmed the choice while fixing the date for the beginning of work. Sometimes he decreed abandonment of the site. Today they have lost this knowledge, as we have. In their modern buildings we do find the H network with its links stretched out, but the knots or crossings are no longer taken into consideration and can be found in full possession of the house.

There was also the possibility of calling upon a lama (a monk with more extensive knowledge), who by a special cere-

Typical Himalayan house and inhabited temple.

mony tried to convince the subterranean power to accept the construction. We would be tempted to say that he thus had the power of neutralizing the effects from underground, as we might try to do by using electronic techniques.

And when these precautions are not observed – the whole country is aware of it – illness is going to strike the occupants of these houses. These observations are as old as the world; we really have discovered nothing in contradiction to that statement.

Once the site has been determined, trenches are dug for the placement of large rocks. The wooden door will be placed before the wall is built, which permits adapting the stone to the irregular contours of the wood. Fine mud is used as a binder in plastering the wall with a conglomerate mix.

It is worth remarking that each house has a room for prayers or its own small chapel, used for intimate worship as well as for receiving the monks who make rounds to give blessings. It is also intended as a private corner for meditation and inner dialogue with the divine.

Life in a large family is a collective life, the important gathering-place being the kitchen. It is the rule to have a hole in the ceiling so as to let the smoke escape; in seeing this arrangement one wonders how it is possible to support it without suffocating.

Once finished, the house is like the Beauty bedecked with a new necklace. It will be decorated with a line of little flags in all colours, attached to a wire strung between two roof beams. This trimming will be affixed during a rising moon and consecrated by a lama. Inscriptions painted on these cloths are the words of Buddha; fluttering in the breeze, they have the function of turning away spirits with evil intentions.

The family sleeps on mats, cushions and rugs. Niches with shelves serve as cupboards. A small alcove serves as washroom, but water is rare.

During the very long winter the kitchen will be the only heated room and everyone comes to sleep there. The other rooms are used for storage and as stables while the cold season persists.

Tradition has it that the entrance is at the east, but in reality it is situated, in most cases and according to our compasses, at the southeast. People say it is less important to sleep with your head at the east than it is to sleep in the direction of a monastery or a stupa. This varies without doubt in relation to their intuitive sensitivity to good vibrations.

It is comprehensible that the inhabitant seeks in his own way to protect himself against the underground deities, who would punish humans by injuring their legs and lower bodies. The cosmic deities strike at the upper body and the region of the head, sometimes leading to madness.

According to these beliefs, the underground deities hibernate so that the awakening of nature in springtime brings with it skin problems. The action of underground energies remains quite fundamental; there is a hierarchy of spirit beings, ranging from those below the earth's surface to those living in the trees, plus the whole gamut of energies at the limits between man and animal and between man and demiurge.

The woman bending over to the ground in her daily work is linked to the earth in a concept of fertility. She will be kept in the background during childbirth, because it is considered to be a polluting act.

The umbilical cord will only be cut two or three days after the birth; during this time the newborn infant continues to be nourished by the placenta. During this period there will be ceremonies to prevent a bad destiny, reminding us of our own fairy stories.

They wait from two months to two years before giving a name to the child, a name chosen and adapted according to the knowledge of the astrologer.

The Tibetan house is inviting; one feels good in it. It relates to a Tibetan greeting which goes like this: "may all living beings be happy", and this is not a trite saying.

Might it not be their harmonious dwelling that gives to its occupants those radiant, smiling expressions?

5. The Living Naga

Symbolically, the Naga is that subterranean serpent which corresponds especially to our underground streams and watercourses. Our contemporary savants may want to attribute this to legend or to a religious belief, but on these

Ritual to appease the Naga and hence cure a sick person of the village.

Himalayan heights the Naga is a reality, a concrete phenomenon with whom one lives day to day, of whom one
speaks, and with whom a dialogue takes place in a most
natural way.

In certain regions this terrestrial impulse is symbolized by
the dragon, and in the Far East they speak of the subterranean crocodile, the Nak.

Between modern geobiology and the very old knowledge of these underground forces there occurred a collision of souls who suddenly came face to face. This was at Alchi in Ladakh. A procession of monks dressed in their dark red robes came down from the village, horns leading and followed by drums and tambourines, to attract the attention of the Naga. The monks headed for the banks of the Indus and anyone ignorant of their purpose might suppose they were going to render homage to the silvery waves of the valley. The monk at the end of the line carried a basin filled with flowers and petals, and he had veiled his face strangely with a bright red cowl. He threw the flowers into the river while the drummers made an enormous noise like the rolling of thunder.

The real reason for this procession was that there was a sick person in the village, whose illness was attributed to the presence of an underground stream passing beneath his bedroom. Periodically his hips locked and that, they said, happened when the Naga became angry. So it was necessary to soothe him by wiping the illness up from the place with flower petals and throwing them in the river.

Because we also know this kind of Naga, we were able to recommend, through intermediaries, that the sick person's bed be moved. All this had to be said, of course, with deep respect for their anxieties and all the while reassuring them that the fact of avoiding the Naga would not provoke his anger anew. It is always a delicate matter to trouble old ghosts.

In the end it is man who makes his choice; Nature herself is indifferent to the decision he takes.

Dialogue with these phenomena is part of everyday life for the inhabitants who have always lived with and observed the laws of greater Nature.

So these Nagas are underground forces and the owners of the land. The scarcity of water explains the importance given to subterranean and aquatic deities linked to fertility. Numerous ceremonies in their honour unfold during the agricultural cycle of the year. Before the harvest and in order to have a good crop the monks go in procession from village to village; they go into meditation playing their sacred music, passing from one house to another and carrying with them the heavy Scriptures of the monastery. These rituals last from one to several days. Once the harvest is in, winter can come. Then comes the season of marriages; the old people prefer to die at the beginning of the big freeze.

In the temple of Giull at Alchi, where all the Buddhas are turned to face south-east (here again, the same direction found in other religions), we note the presence of the great Goruda who tames two Nagas.

Here, as under the feet of Christ at Chartres, the gods do not allow themselves to get intertwined. In the sub-basement there is a confusion of deformed silhouettes, animals and spirits who have dozens of complicated names. Some of them, with their frightful teeth, devour the underground passions. Goruda, who eats the tails of dragon-serpents, is considered the vehicle, the chariot of Vishnu. Although some deny it, the relations and inter-actions with Hinduism are constant; the vibrations rein-force the case, being reproducible at 14,000 units in both doctrines.

Nagas which have been disturbed – whether by a badly-organized structure, by polluted waters or by having been frustrated in some other way – must be appeased. Everyone is drawn into it, it is a collective activity, for the difficulties of daily life, illness, accidents, drought and flood are all attributed to the Nagas.

Fish are not eaten because they are linked to the world of the Nagas.

The traditional sacred dances are part of the ritual during monastic ceremonies and festivities. During the festival of Taktok, for example, all the deities make a pompous entrance with their masks, both beatific and terrifying. Each in turn performs a dance with very slow gestures and movements, each expressing by precise signs his individual message. These gestures were and still are a language in these Asiatic holy places.

One of the monk dancers attracts our attention because he carries a fat Naga under his arm. We would like to understand better these ritual gestures expressing, sym-bolically, a way to re-establish equilibrium between heaven and earth. He carries on his back four little red flags which relate to the four points of the compass.

The green Naga.

The god Goruda, in the temple of Giull at Alchi, will not let the two Nagas get tangled up.

These studied gestures of the religious dances are related to a ritual which seeks identification with the divine. It tries to capture energies in movement; it hopes to restore harmony where there is disorder, the separated elements coming together again by affinity.

It is the same thing with our Western Nagas. Only we are adapting a more technical language to the vagaries of underground watercourses. Yesterday's observation can be interesting and useful for understanding that of tomorrow, as is true of all research.

6. Symphony at Dawn

It is six o'clock in the morning in the monastery of Lamayuru. We are at 3600 metres (11,800 feet), surrounded by a cirque of extraordinary cliffs.

It is prayer time at the break of a chilly day. The strong, chanting voice of the monk in a dark red cassock can appear to be, for the visitor, a monotonous litany. But we are going to follow the nuances of these vibrations with the biometer and study the impact that the chanted rhythm has on the body. You can let yourself be lulled without understanding the words, but it is clear that the crashing blows of the tambourines have not left our adrenalin indifferent. The initiates know this.

The performer himself may well be ignorant of the significance of his rhythmic reading, but he is master of the ritual's programme. The pendulum begins to dance above the biometer, vibrating as if it were itself the sacred game. It is sensitive to all the nuances, in such a way that the vibratory tonalities almost become written music. There is a real diffusion of subtle waves penetrating our physical and etheric bodies.

This musical meditation unfolds in four well-organized sequences:

1. In the beginning, during the first ten minutes, the physical must meld with the vibration of the place; this necessary time of adaptation is recognized and is measurable by cutaneous resistance and the geo-rhythmogram. It is a matter of relaxing and creating inner emptiness, letting this sonorous and inhabitual language reach us. During this lapse of time the biometer indicates nothing of significance, but once caught up in the harmony of the affair our physical energy starts to soar.

2. Little by little, our own vibrations begin to keep time with the prayer, and then! . . . the shattering blow of the cymbal strikes not only the nervous system at the same instant but it immediately provokes a recharging of physical energy which will hold at 8000 to 10,000 units until the end of the third phase of the ceremony.

    The rolling sound creates a kind of momentary tension, the shot in the arm which stings.

3. As the prayer is pronounced at a slower rhythm we register a lowering of vibrations, a calming hollow in the wave. But the rhythm of the cymbal blows is progressively accelerated and at each stroke it is as if

95

our physical body was being bombarded by unknown particles of nearly insupportable vibrations of 9000 to 11,000 units, following one after the other. This level is the bridge making the connection to our etheric body. We remain thus, suspended at that high vibration for a lapse of time; it holds us prisoner until the moment when, like a sword stroke of words coming faster and faster and a waterfall of tambourines, we come down to earth.

The physical level is now magnificently in equilibrium at 8000 units, and the energetic level signals to us the 13,500 vibrations obtained by this ritual.

How good we feel, light and alert! A real therapy!

4. For the finale there follows a kind of recapitulation of the prayers, a sort of rapid checking off of the essential passages previously read in detail. It is like varnish applied to a master painting, putting some finishing touches on the fresh harmony of our physical and etheric bodies. For half an hour there are boosts and peaks of vibrations up to 11,000.

At the end it is as if a blessing has been proposed to us: "Go in the strength you have"! (Judges 6:14)

If that dawn symphony has penetrated into a deep sector of our subconscious, it could be that one day it will make us dream or cry.

The interior of the Lamayuru temple is also free of any telluric network. But a point of concentrated terrestrial power gushes from the spot where the monk diffused his energizing prayer. He was seated on five crossing-points of H rays, a point of power and emission that would make a small menhir jealous. A broadcasting point of this type maintains the entire environment in an etheric current, and at Lamayuru it measures 13,500 units. One must add that the vibratory prayer is renewed every day by the monks' ritual. Thus these privileged few of "another world" can benefit from the subtleness of emitted vibrations which influence the physical and energetic bodies. Their health at this power point is further sustained by 30 microroentgens of radioactivity, the highest rate measured on these high plateaux of the Indus.

Reading of the prayer.

It is surprising that, in these Tibetan temples in general, the vibrations are maintained only at the physical and etheric levels. That third dimension, the spiritual presence, is only rarely perceptible. At Lamayuru there is only the small holy meditation spot of Naropa which registers a higher vibration. But is this not what the Buddhist philosophy wants, whether at the terrestrial or the human level, that bliss will enter into the quietness of the heart? It is said that the most precious thing, the only thing that counts, is to gain the peace of the heart, rather than to get tangled up in the swamp of bitter and useless individual experiences.

The Buddhist wants a better life now and not tomorrow. He remains on the plane of Compassion; like a light tinged with love for one's neighbour, it wins the people and the monks. It is only the eminent Sage who can be part of the

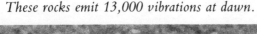

These rocks emit 13,000 vibrations at dawn.

elite and still know how to practise complete detachment from all things.

Those stones which also express themselves at dawn
Who can easily admit that there is life in a pebble or a rock? Their molecular structure remains locked into divided formulas; stone is classified in a general way as inert matter.

Let us place an oscilloscope and a biometer on a stone from the Himalayan desert. In the morning we will measure vibrations with a value of 3000 Bovis units and in the afternoon it will be 4000.

This difference could be explained by correlation with the daily rhythm: in the morning the sun gives energies and the earth takes them, and in the afternoon it is just the opposite, the earth giving and the sun taking. Besides, it is easily noticed that we feel extremely tired with exposure to the afternoon sun.

But what a revelation, which would remain unbelievable if other researchers on other sites had not also observed this phenomenon: a Tibetan rock bearing the sacred inscription

Om mane padme hum

and which gives off vibrations of 3000 and 4000 units during the day, begins to vibrate at 13,000 units at dawn!

Might it not be those stones placed by the thousands on tombs and stupas which will help the deceased to pass in vibratory harmony that period of 49 days called the bardo? The Tibetans believe that this intermediate state follows death and is composed of seven periods of seven days.

Whatever we might know about this, it would doubtless be more reassuring at the moment of demise to benefit from a prayer chanted at a vibration adapted to the situation, as a lama knows how to do. The etheric body would then undergo its transfer from the physical body in greater harmony.

What really is cruelly lacking in the technology of our dehumanized hospitals is a "someone" who helps the other to die.

These vibrations of love – because they do exist – deserve to be decoded and diffused throughout the world like light waves. But on our wavelengths, whether short or medium, there is only futile blabbering.

We are far from the vibratory symphony of dawn at

Lamayuru. Let us place this monastery geographically: after having crossed the pass of Fatu-la at an altitude of 4091 metres (13,422 feet) you plunge into a cirque of fantastic ochre rocks. It is on this site that we have registered the highest radioactivity of the northern chain of Ladakh. A beautiful legend recounts that in days gone by a large lake occupied the bottom of the valley. A disciple of Ananda, the faithful companion of Buddha, came through the air prophesying the establishment of a monastery. Offering some grains of barley to the Nagas, he slashed the mountain as if with a sword blow but using only his spiritual power. Water surged from the breach and arable land was placed at man's disposal.

At Lamayuru at six o'clock in the morning there is prayer before sunrise, a prayer not like the others.

7. *Are Prayer Wheels only Wind?*

In several religious environments, but especially in the Tibetan tradition, the prayer wheel is supposed to contain an energizing formula. That is precisely what intrigued us.

The initiate would say that in putting the prayer wheel into movement he establishes contact between the microcosm and the macrocosm. Because this great man possesses knowledge and serves as a model for the people, he cannot be challenged. The prayer wheel holds one or more prayers or mantras, inscribed in beautiful calligraphy on parchments or cloths which are carefully rolled inside it. The words are nearly always the usual "Om mane padme hum", which will be diffused relentlessly as long as one continues to turn the wheel. This silent wheel is supposed to be the receptacle of a sacred force, sealed into the written word. When it is activitated it will have a beneficial influence.

Watching certain old monks who were trying to keep alert during a very long ceremony, it was interesting to note that when they felt tired and their posture seemed to sag, they took their prayer wheels and set them to turning, always revolving clockwise. We never failed to see the bodies straighten up in a joyous spirit.

Is energy really provided, or is the belief in it the best placebo?

Typical prayer wheel.

It may be that these people are more open to receiving the emission of a prayer wheel, for our repeated efforts with the object and the biometer did not directly modify the vitality of the physical body. But – an astonishing thing – it did augment energy at the level of the etheric body. Physical strength would thus be affected and increased by inter-action.

And when we amuse ourselves by turning the prayer wheel above our heads, always clockwise, we feel the same boost in well-being that comes from a massage or the hands of a magnetizer.

Let he who doubts try, on the contrary, to proceed with spinning it in the opposite direction – counterclockwise – and with surprise he will discover, as will especially his dog, that this is not simply "hot air".

The Westerner, with his condescending glance, will have trouble in grasping these other value systems which are realities for the local people and help them to live. The lamas always received us and our questions amiably, keeping a smile which could mask their thoughts and their secret feelings.

For us, the prayer wheel resting motionless in its niche or its tabernacle is only an unpretentious object. It merits admiration when it is made of chased copper, such as are certain models from the eighteenth century, or when it is in beautiful lustrous wood or covered with old leather. But we are a little shocked, and it is understandable, by the sight of some prayer wheels made from old vegetable tins still bearing the manufacturer's label.

In front of prayer drums, when they are stationary, the biometer shows us only the vitality of the place. The prayer wheel, once put into motion, will make the environment vibrate immediately up to 12,000 and 13,000 units. Each passerby, whether conscious of it or not, will doubtless have received his drop of etheric refreshment. If he is withdrawn and insensitive he will notice nothing except a smarting under the eyelids.

One has to admit that the formula "Om mani padme hum" is pronounced on any occasion and most of the time people are ignorant of its meaning. It means "The All is a precious jewel in the lotus flower which blooms in my heart"; this is the allegory of the mandala. This centre, this jewel, is the Buddha in meditation.

Do not forget the innumerable little flags and cloths ranged from length of poles bearing inscriptions of prayers and sacred words. These fluttering cloths deteriorate rapidly with wind and weather and must be renewed often.

A flag in perfect condition and in movement can influence its environment and, by the quantity of vibrations created, influence the etheric body as well. Everything becomes vibration-life. But the faded flag, even in movement, has lost all its impact. The only thing that passes is the sigh of the wind.

There are Tibetan monks living on certain power points who are so-called illiterates. How does it happen then that, suddenly, they begin to speak several modern languages or know how to read fluently very old Latin or Greek texts?

This is quite troubling. Is it a Pentecostal force where each one linked to the divine flame will speak in a different tongue? Might one suspect that these monks, beneath their apparent good-naturedness, harbour that incredible capacity of identification which is latent at every instant in universal communication? For he who knows how to perceive it, a quiet force emanates from their beings, impregnated with the vibration of the sacred place.

But it is not given to everyone to meet them . . .

—————— CHAPTER 6 ——————

Chartres

1. The Eloquence of Chartres

Aside from all that has been said and written on the subject of
the cathedral of Chartres, geobiology uncovers and adds
some titbits.

The northeast orientation of the edifice is well known,
being adapted to the trace of the underground watercourse
which traverses it. Other structures of the same type have also
been placed with reference to, firstly, the effect of underground water and then in relation to compass points.

At Chartres it is sufficient to observe, outside the cathedral,
how the trees growing above the watercourse are covered
with moss up to their branches: this permanent humidity rises
by capillary action. At a distance of 15 metres (49 feet) from
the edifice, on the south-west side, a large fault of about 80
centimetres (2 feet 7 inches) wide must certainly play a not
inconsiderable role in the site's influence. The question arises:
may there not be an analogy with the famous H barrier
around the Egyptian temples?

Water is also found everywhere under the religious sites of
the West, where the allegory of the serpent – here the
"wivern" – is brought to the fore. The influence of the Celts,
who were once Scandinavians, is also rediscovered at
Chartres, which prides itself on having the largest known
Gothic vault. Celtic and Druidic symbols play hide-and-seek
in this power point, the most remarkable in France's constel-
lation of cathedrals as well as in the entire network of holy
places as far as Santiago de Compostela. Originally the image
of Christ on the cross appeared nowhere. Why then tirelessly
project a tortured and tormented body on that target which is
the believer? In the end he is no longer impressed by it.
Superabundance leads to indifference, while the conception of
the initiate-builders was evidence of respect and glory for a
house of God in which one worshipped exclusively a living
spirit, the true transcendence.

The naked cross would thus become even more indisputably the image of his teaching, emphasizing the eternal relationship between Earth and Heaven, where verticality fixes the line of the qualitative and the elevating, while horizontality determines that of the quantitative and the surface. In the vertical we come back to the words "but seek first his kingdom" (Matthew 6:33) and only then comes the horizontal, proposing the two arms opened wide to humanity. In addition, the crucifix only appears from the beginning of the twelfth century. In order to establish the shape of the base of the cathedrals, the cross was schematically fixed to the ground and represents the pentagram, in which the human body can be seen in the abstract.

At all times there has been attributed to Chartres the force of a place where man is susceptible to feel that energy, even if he is a non-believer. There have been efforts to explain that power of impregnation uniquely by the presence of telluric currents, which remain rather vague in contemporary terminology. This cathedral is more than a simple monument of knowledge; this entity of stone behaves like a physical body, it is the material support of an etheric body belonging to the edifice. The whole is nourished both by a permanent impulse coming from the power of the site and by a cosmic impulse which has been skilfully captured.

This is what attracts us and what surpasses us.

Within the choir enclosure the surface between the stalls is free of H rays and neutral without any crossing-point. Additionally, our measurements indicate a natural neutralization of the zone which can be, without doubt, related to an effect of the stained-glass windows which filter the cosmic rays and create a wavelength adequate to harmonize with human cells.

The arrangement of water channels arriving at a precise point in the centre of the choir contributes largely to the influence of the site from below. The builders knew how to avoid H network crossing-points in this zone. We know from geobiology that, in such a case, the human being standing on these telluric knots has much difficulty in concentrating.

This underground current of water is symbolized everywhere by the serpent; at Chartres it is called the wivern. Let us examine the south-east portal: one of the most beautiful sculptures imaginable, showing Christ grave and grandiose, resigned across the centuries to see pass through this entry both fervent and half-hearted believers. In one hand he holds the sealed book of the greatest Revelation of all time.

The three starting-points of the builder-templars were precisely this revelation, combining classic (Greek) intelligence with the Celtic matter, the tradition, and the ritual.

Under the feet of the Christ is found an allegory for the two terrestrial rays: the two serpents advance from both sides but under Christ's power they cannot intersect. The initiate of the building thus underscores the ability to neutralize these intersections by a force, whatever be the name given to it.

The statue reveals the possible superiority of a spiritual influence over a terrestrial dynamic which often slips stealthily beneath our feet.

2. Hard Knocks for the H Network

The choir at Chartres is a little universe all its own. The music of the elements, harmoniously assembled by the anonymous builders, vibrates in the form of disciplined movements. Those monks who constructed this edifice must have been continually in dialogue with their invisible lines. Plato knew better than we when he said that souls, before descending into bodies, had heard and remembered the celestial concerts.

Here philosophy merges at the summit with mathematics; those great architects mocked neither the mysteries of alchemy nor astrology nor all the sciences of assembled stone. These blocks reaching toward heaven seem to do it with a mobilized power, by a thrust of which man is the initiator. However, there are those who do not hear the music.

In the choir, away from the noise of the world, it ought to be that the H network creates no disturbance. In effect, this chosen and privileged zone is neutral, completely free of Hartmann lines and knots. These lines are pushed away in the four directions, and between the choir and the faithful we find them concentrated in a bundle which lets the communications pass but which subtly protects the ecclesiastics.

So this H network was conceived from the outset in such a way that the concentrations of lines were situated in the

Chartres Cathedral: Statue of Christ above the wiverns which do not quite touch.

perimeter of the choir; they had to pass behind the stalls. The high ecclesiastical dignitaries must have felt as if in a cocoon, but this privilege only lasted until the eighteenth century! We made this striking observation: these provocative, even aggressive, lines now pass right across two rows of choir stalls!

We do believe that the well-informed builders did not wish it so. Then what happened?

In this case, within the structure of a systematic search for causes, we can only suppose it to be due to the way in which renovations were organized during the following centuries, accomplished unfortunately without science and without conscience.

Even if alchemy still has not acquired its credentials, we can only bow in admiration before the stained-glass windows of Chartres. They are exceptional, for the stone has been hollowed out and the stained-glass inserted. These minerals have a neutralizing action which modifies the oscillating circuit, acting in a frequency modulation of gigahertz dimensions. Colour plays an obvious complementary role, and certain ancient wise men claimed that these windows were conceived so as to hold back the luminous particles which are harmful to initiation. In fact, we are really penetrated by an energy whose name is unknown.

The construction was originally conceived in a harmony of all the elements and parameters. Why was the H network contracted like a dried prune so as to slice through the calm at the level of the stalls? Digging a little into the history of the place, we learn that two stained-glass windows to the left and the right of the choir were replaced in the eighteenth century by large clear windows, which are still there today. It is shocking to discover that these magnificent high windows, as luminous at nightfall as in full sun, were destroyed on the order of Bishop Bridan during the 1770s, so that the faithful could admire him better in full light!

In any case, this change was simply a crime, and we cannot often enough repeat to those in charge of these sacred edifices: be careful during transformations, the Knowledge was here!

In parentheses
The heart contracts also when one penetrates into Notre Dame of Paris. For more than a half-century this cathedral has

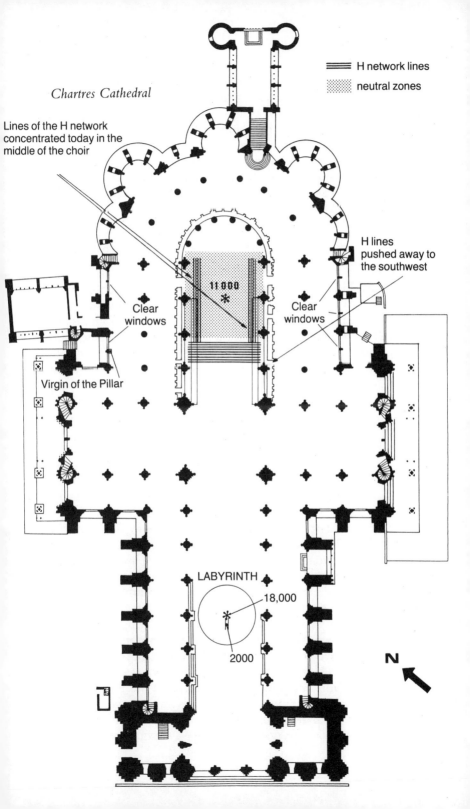

Chartres Cathedral

Lines of the H network concentrated today in the middle of the choir

H network lines

neutral zones

H lines pushed away to the southwest

11 000
*

Clear windows

Clear windows

Virgin of the Pillar

LABYRINTH

18,000

2000

N

been martyrized by hostile works, ordered by ignorant intellectuals and more harmful than the erosion. They have crammed electric cables into gaping trenches, and these are the modern wiverns, plump and plasticized, which are creating the new microclimate of Notre Dame! Entering there tomorrow, are we going to find a few crumbs of that sacred feeling, or will there only remain of that book of stone a dusty sunset? There as well, torture has not yet been abolished!

3. A Touch of Ecstasy

This choir with its boundaries so carefully delineated was also thought to be a vault of protection for the learned man, who sought to render living and present an invisible holiness. That strange feeling of identification with a spiritual Intelligence cannot develop in man just anywhere.

There, in the centre of the choir where fourteen subterranean watercourses curiously converge – whose details are noted below in Section Seven and its accompanying plan – there is a precise point equidistant between the top of the gothic vault and the underground water (about 37 metres) (121 feet) which gives the individual an impression of weightlessness. There is a vertical line which, like a carrying wave, permits man to feel this little nothing which takes possession of space. In an essay on ancient knowledge, in relation to the medicine of Aesculapius, it is said: two things in parallel determine a line of influence halfway between them. A force line appears according to this orientation.

The Earth gave Chartres a unique gift. This site raises man to a point of etheric enhancement. It is like a state of grace, it is there that the priest must stand. The subject of the ancient site is controversial; what is certain is that the altar has been moved. In its new position there is an emission of shape-related waves that has nothing in common with the old location, which was without parallel and clearly desired by the builders. The biometer registers 11,000 vibratory units in the old position (indicated by an asterisk on the illustration).

This power point in a holy place is accentuated by the large loop in the underground river and by the complicity of the 14 channels bringing water. Once again we find the principle of varied crossing-points: the water, the gothic design, and the stone all in tension with one another.

That extraordinary sensation is only produced on this point if a person remains standing; the horizontal wave of the Hartmann structure thus passes at the level of his solar plexus and his upraised arms. At ground level the effect disappears. So only a standing person will be able to taste the exaltation, comparable to what is felt when arriving on the summit of a high mountain.

Can our contemporary priest still grant himself the privilege of being able to soar deliberately above common mortals? He will often be obliged, in calling upon the vibrations of higher laws, to apply them against inferior conditions.

The loop in this underground stream and one arm of the channels fanning out under the cathedral also supply the well of Saint-Forts. What a significant name. Two power points of water coincide there; its water is said to have therapeutic value and that provides the force, the "forts". Why not? This same water, also used for all initiatory rituals, can thus lead to both health and holiness . . .

It is as if a birthplace for two great qualities were proposed at the edge of a well.

4. *The Sleeping Labyrinth*

The labyrinth of a cathedral is composed of a series of concentric circles, interrupted at certain points in such a way as to create a bizarre and inextricable itinerary.

The essential quality that stands out is the complexity of its plan and the difficulty of its route. The complicated pathways are thus intended to delay the traveller's arrival at the centre. Access to the centre, at the end of a kind of initiatory journey, was forbidden to those who were not qualified. In a way it also symbolizes and substitutes for a pilgrimage to the Holy Land. The believer who could not accomplish the real pilgrimage travelled the labyrinth until he arrived at his goal. Thus the pilgrim staying close to home may even do it on his knees over a distance, on the labyrinth of Chartres, of about two hundred metres.

At Chartres the labyrinth is a design of stones laid into the paved floor; two colours are used, grey-white and a greenish black. The public does not always notice it, because from the principal entry there is a sea of chairs covering a large part of this circle. There was a ritual for covering this route embedded in the floor: in certain regions one danced over it with bare feet. Our shoes make a screen.

All around the labyrinth we find a vibration of 6500 units, which is nothing special, but starting from the entry-point in the lines of this one we are bathed in an equilibrating vibration of 8000 units. Inside the loops, where the local magnetic field can quicken one's step, we are brought to the higher vibratory level of the etheric body at 13,500 units. The goal is to penetrate to the centre of the labyrinth while charged with a maximum of a sort of static electricity which one's passage has accumulated by friction. And there, at the last step before the centre, how astonished we are to see the vibrations fall abruptly to 2000. This passage weakens your knees. But we have to know how to fall, to drop, in order to understand farther on the leap of Joy.

The intensity is surprising in the centre: 18,000 units, which corresponds to a Pharaoh's initiation point!

This labyrinth was an initiatory path which risked remaining only an old dream that one would have liked to prolong in time. One is rather like a timid child who is careful not to go astray. However it is not the tourist, passing by rapidly, who will be sanctified.

Other conceptions have made of the labyrinth a symbolic prototype of our brain. Arriving at the centre, one is surrounded by six semicircular lobes where human thoughts circulate and among which one can get lost.

Does that foreshadow the developmental stages of our soul in twice three degrees?

Thus at the centre there is a white stone, a battery for accumulating the Earth-Cosmos current and where the being, his energy dispersed by a multitide of desires, reintegrates his lost unity. A science such as this cannot be improvised.

5. The Virgin of the Pillar

She is one of the mysteries of Chartres and, today as well as yesterday, she gives and strikes when she wishes.

This is not the Black Virgin, but she is just as dark; she

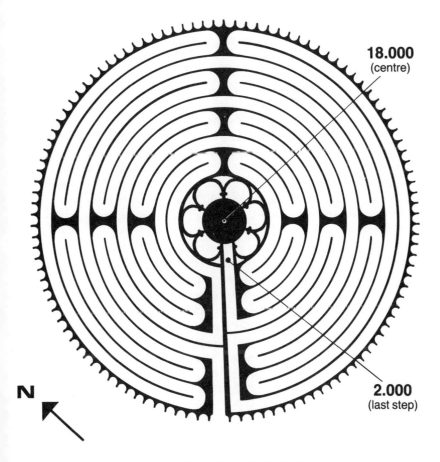

18.000
(centre)

2.000
(last step)

N

Labyrinth of the Cathedral of Chartres

dates from the fifteenth century and is an object of great veneratlon.

This point of the cathedral is unusual and precipitated us into an astonishing and unexpected experience.

Within the limited zone in front of the Virgin, where the prayer benches are found, there is already a high intensity of 9000 units. This is a vibration which always has a very strong impact on the physiological system. The georhythmogram also shows an Important variation, compared to other zones of the paving-stone floor.

This intensity is not always well tolerated by certain people; they feel themselves to be in a general state of nervous excitement. What can there be immediately next to the Virgin of the Pillar that is so special? When approaching on foot one may be shaken by a shudder, the next person is moved to flee suddenly, children will enter this zone only if dragged by their mother's hand and then they cry . . .

Something is happening. The vibration is especially low, less than 1000, which is comparable to falling, to going momentarily into a deathlike state. It is even a point where one is sucked downward before crossing the next threshold. And all around us faces are twisted, appearing to wish desperately for a thread of hope to cling to. The atmosphere of the place is totally tense, and yet a holy place should, on the contrary, erase worry and let peace smooth our expressions.

The question arises if we might not be on one of those points where the initiate-builders could have concealed catalysts of energy in the skeleton of the cathedral. . . .

This evident and incomprehensible aggressiveness in a renowned site intrigued us. We decided to try to stay within this precise radiation as long as it might be supportable. Several of us began to feel more and more ill, empty, beaten, and when the tension and the headaches became intolerable, we took flight from that infernal trap.

Nothing very objective so far, one could retort. And yet, when we got out into the fresh air we looked at one another wide-eyed: our skin was as if burned. There had doubtless been a strong defensive reaction of the epidermis; it could be said that we had almost adopted the pigmentation of the statue. This might still seem improbable if we had not had, in other circumstances, an identical experience following some tests, done in an incompetent way, with that still-untamed energy whose smallest particles are called tachyons.

According to American, Russian, Australian and Japanese researchers the concentration of this field of energy approaches 880 million volts per centimetre. At this point we do not want to anticipate the theme of the poorly-understood energy which is discussed in the final chapter. What can be said is that the curious researcher or the willing guinea pig risk paying dearly for treating as a game what is serious and even fearsome.

Our measurements made before this precise point of the

Virgin can be compared, in violence, with those that can be registered in front of a colour television set.

The Virgin of the Pillar is not innocent.

We, knowing very little of initiatory methods, of those influences sought by those who possess the Knowledge, have perhaps somewhat disturbed the myth of the All-Sublime that one would expect to find in a holy place.

Chartres really seems to be still in possession of certain mysteries.

Dark passageways are doubtless necessary in order to appreciate the light. But there are also customs and rituals which kill. In this respect it is recommended not to play with laws that one does not know.

Such a surprising and painful experience in a power point can only carry the label "interpretation incomplete".

6. Coaxing the Truth from a Legend

There is no resisting the attraction of old stories and sayings, and they often contain a grain of truth.

According to legend, and also according to the historian Froissart, the King of England's army laid siege to the city of Chartres in 1360. Edward III had installed his camp near Brétigny, about five kilometres away. It seems that one morning, under blue skies, he gave the order to attack, and suddenly, although nothing would have led one to expect it, a terrible storm broke just above the camp. The story has it that such "large stones" fell, as hail, that men and horses were killed.

The horrified King then raised his arms in the direction of the cathedral towers, imploring Notre Dame to put an end to this disaster in exchange for a promise of peace with France. And miracle there was, for the tempest ended.

We simply had to go and take a look at this old army encampment, and it was surprising to discover that even today a vast uncluttered countryside permits us to plunge into the geographic configuration of the time. From Brétigny at the south-east of Chartres, as the crow flies and without obstacle, one still sees the two towers of the cathedral behind the hills. They stick up like real antennae.

About a kilometre to the east, between Brétigny and

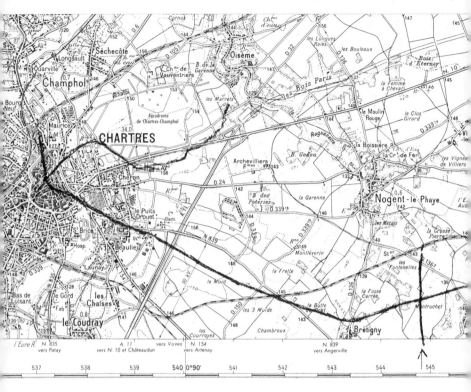

Intersection of streams at Brétigny, with one leading to Chartres

Chandres, we found the group of fields which should be where the army camped. Why there?

Beneath this site two large subterranean streams cross at two different depths. One of them is the one which passes under the cathedral of Chartres; so it is in direct relation with the terrestrial magnetic field which follows the course of the underground water. The wivern is still chasing us.

It is known that lightning nearly always concentrates on places where watercourses are found stacked and intersecting. It even seems that as the vertical distance between two streams becomes greater, the terrestrial magnetic field becomes more powerful, creating a favoured target for violent lightning.

These same geophysical phenomena are observable at places where highway accidents seem always to occur at the same spot, supposedly for unexplainable reasons. More

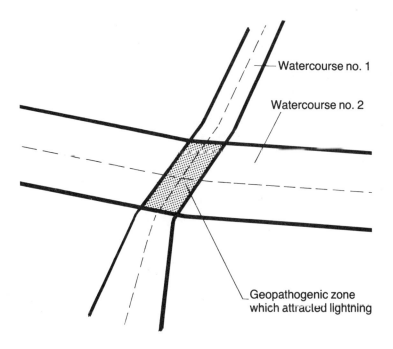

than two thousand files have been established on this subject.

The warriors camped near Chartres had therefore chosen a place above the crossing of two large underground streams, which justified the hypothesis that lightning would be strongly attracted to the site.

The King – could he have been an initiated king? With two arms raised to the sky, did he not create two transmitters directed toward two receiving antennae? These, in their turn, could modify the zone's vibratory field. That is really what we do today, simply using other kinds of transmitters.

The question thus arises if Jesus did not use these same laws and these same powers to calm the storm which threatened to capsize his boat. We can allow ourselves to be Doubting Thomases, for a certain scepticism renders service to a society strewn with fanatics.

There do exist subtle techniques in this business of wave emission, and they are not always used for the good of mankind. There are still others which we ignore deliberately in refusing to apply them at higher levels. Even so, we should not cast aspersions on man's capacities just because we do not want to know about them.

Among the eccentricities manifested in the clouds we might take note that some of our grandfathers saw an aurora borealis at our latitudes in June 1914. For them there was no doubt that this was an omen presaging war. They had no radio and they did not know what was brewing.

Have there been other cosmic signs of human thought clusters?

In the tradition of the North American Indians the hurricane is conceived as a conspiracy of three elements:

air, fire, water . . . against the Earth.

Numerous legends make mention of the intemperance of cosmic energies, of the revolt of the elements. What do we really know about it? Meteorology and Mythology have been good partners.

Yesterday in the service of the King – tomorrow the servants of science may simply replace the word mythology.

7. Similarity and Difference

There was reason to be astonished at the underground structure and the arrival of 14 regular streams – arranged like a fan – under the choir of the cathedral of Chartres.

It would appear to be improbable that Nature alone could have put together such a scheme. For a very long time we guessed that such a situation must be one of a kind. There is such regularity in the progress of these underground water systems. Is it believable that chance was the accomplice of the constructors, supporting their extensive knowledge?

What we needed was the surprising comparison with the identical layout of the choir of the cathedral of Santiago de Compostela, the better to close in on the truth. For there we got an unexpected answer.

Fourteen streams arrive under the choir of the cathedral of Chartres, and so it is that in the cathedral of Compostela the identical regular structures are found, directed and gathered together in the same way beneath the choir! These water inflows are made conspicuous in the paving of the

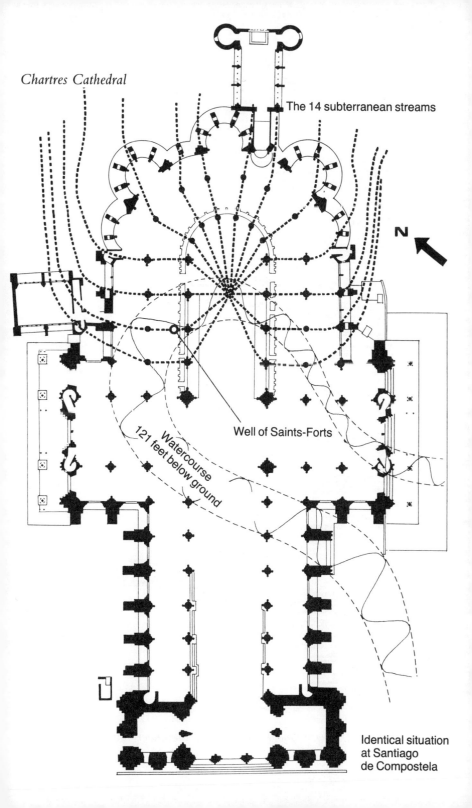

Chartres Cathedral

The 14 subterranean streams

N

Well of Saints-Forts

Watercourse
121 feet below ground

Identical situation
at Santiago
de Compostela

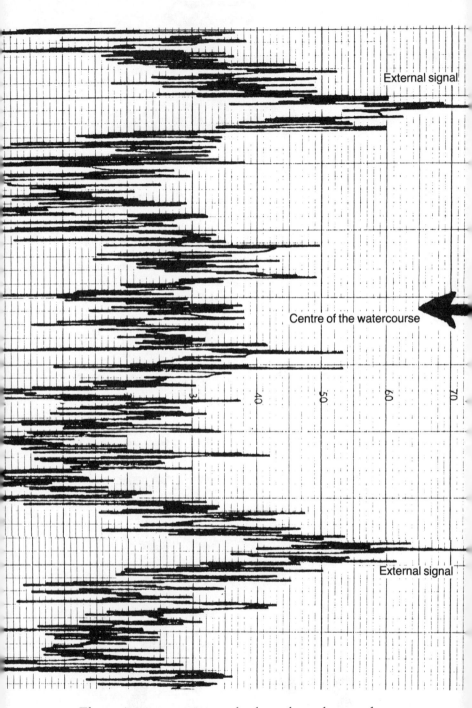

Electronic measurements made above the underground streams

side corridors – one could say they are signalled – by 14 wide inlays of black marble. During the decade of the 1960s there were large excavations under the cathedral of Santiago de Compostela, and what did they find?

These old inflow channels had been dug by human hands.

So at Chartres it is not a caprice of Nature, nor pure happenstance, nor the hand of the gods, but truly the omniscience of the builders.

8. *Compostela loses a Star*

But there you are: today, at Compostela the channels are dry! Urban renewal work executed in the nearby quarter of the old city required a modification of the water distribution system, that esoteric contribution which is indispensable to support the vibration necessary to condition our cells.

Large iron-mesh reinforcements were set in concrete in order to strengthen the foundations of the edifice. Still more reinforced concrete was used to consolidate the base of the flooring. But what especially hurt, as a consequence of these works executed between 1948 and 1968, was that the subterreanean water passages, programmed by the constructors, were cut.

It is often said that since then there are no more miracles at Santiago de Compostela.

The great Star of Compostela has been eclipsed, has been extinguished for ever.

This warning cannot be repeated too often: it is important neither to add nor to subtract just anything in just any old way, wherever transformations are necessary in a place where the sacred knowledge of the Ancients had been applied.

9. *Virgins of the Earth*

In the basement of the cathedral of Chartres these 14 streams are symbolized by seven doves around the Black Virgin (the earth), each dove having two beaks ($2\times7=14$).

This Virgin is also known by the name of Notre Dame of Beneath-the-Earth and she is also called the "virgin of the druids". The stone used expresses itself through its polarity; when it is well-placed, in a good location, it is the black stone of "Isis". "Is" means sacred, it is the sacred thing, the sacred place.

Black is not really her colour; it is the definition of the influence which is expressed in this place. It is that which gave birth to the Black Virgin of Chartres and to the black stone of Arafat.

Thus, in any sacred place, a black virgin will be found. This will always be in relation with the influence of the place and the underground water.

The merit of the cathedral builders is to have known how to bring all these elements together so as to create cosmo-telluric power points.

We can salute them for having been the first geobiologists of the gothic era.

CHAPTER 7

Santiago de Compostela

1. A River of Holiness

The custom of the time stimulates a desire to follow the great names of history in trying to relive, in our day, the famous moments of a power point.

Alas, water no longer flows beneath the choir of Compostela. The flooring and the new concrete spans have combined to maintain a permanent barrier, as much for those still to be born as for the present generation.

But is that a sufficient pretext to assert that there are no more miracles at Santiago de Compostela?

Certainly not. Above the solemn faces there is also a very high vibration-light that we need luck to catch on the wing, like a flash of lightning that one might capture in a fraction of a second. But it could also completely escape us.

The large silver statue of St. James gleams above the crypt where the saint's urn lies. This figure is placed very high and is either too visible or impossible to see if you approach too closely. The visitor or pilgrim who passes by rapidly will retain only the impression of a collective feeling.

But there also exist moments of grace when the thinking of the surprised seeker dissolves in light, under an almost physical form of sparks crackling around his head.

Terrible rationalists that we are, we measured on the Bovis scale a vibration never before attained on a power point.

The pilgrim can climb by a narrow stairway up to shoulder level of the saint's statue, as seen from the back. There, exactly vertically above the crypt where the apostle's remains rest, is produced the extraordinary shock of 21,000 units! This is the threshold of the Unknown. How does it happen that above that tomb should be this light of life, illuminating the brain, dazzling and transporting the human being above the clouds? It is as if our heads suddenly became light and illuminated, leaving behind a doughy body and entering into a multitude of translucid diamond bubbles, reflecting iridescent colours.

We would like to be able to understand and deepen the meaning of this marvellous blossoming. Is it Pure Energy, an instant of flight in the Overconscious which plays at hide-and-seek? Or is it a contact of the "I" of the Saint with the small "me" who passes by, even across the ages . . .?

A unique and fabulous instant in the life of man, an instant of incomparable richness. A favour certainly, but also a kind of unexpected miracle!

It would be fine if every human being could, once in his life, plunge into such a brilliant instant, and that is really what the pilgrim hopes for. However, in observing man in the mass, who seems to have lost his individuality, we can only be saddened to see him locked tightly in the opaque density of his own reality. But let us hope that without noticing it his physical presence will even so have intercepted some reflections of holiness. There are often some crumbs which fall from the table without our noticing it.

2. The Baptistry Dethroned

In the middle of the ambulatory, behind the giant statue of St. James, we are brought down to earth, surrounded by exuberant rococo decorations. One of the most beautiful of the original baptistries has been placed there, where four streams flow in the direction of the choir. This spot has been chosen, for it coincides with a crossing-point of the Hartmann network and a telluric diagonal crossing. The terrestrial forces of the site were thus brought to maximum concentration for this act linked to the divine: baptism.

In other identical circumstances these noble conch-shell decorations have a vibration of 8000 units, reaching a strong physical level, as well as 13,500 units for consecrating the etheric envelope of the person being baptized. But here at Compostela our biometer falls to its lowest level. The inner works of the point's power no longer function. A heavy iron cover has been sealed over the font with an imposing padlock; a large slot in this cover invites the passer-by to empty his wallet. We have to accept that all religions have in common this need to collect funds, but one questions the need to remove from its pedestal a work of art destined to give holy water and convert it into a beggar.

We wonder what can man gain by knocking off his feet these sensitive points of a sacred edifice, which become like frustrated chakras that one has suffocated.

3. The Pilgrim's Symbol

The clamshell is a motif found at every streetcorner in Compostela. Many details confirm that this symbol is very respected and honoured. An example is a water pipe installed on the façade of an old house: the pipework above the door detours around the shell sculpted into the wall. An irregular installation is preferred to the obliteration of a decoration, and this one has been respectfully kept in its original place.

Why is a shell the symbol of the pilgrims who have come to Compostela over the centuries? It seems the explanation is quite matter-of-fact: it is simply that the pilgrims nourished themselves with the excellent shellfish of the region. The "coquille Saint-Jacques" has become famous on our tables. So they attached an empty shell to their clothing as a souvenir.

However we would also take poetic pleasure in linking this shell to the significance given it by the Aztecs: it is the womb, the birth, the moon presiding at the birth of vegetation and life. The moon being bound to the earth, we rediscover the exchange of life in its cosmo-terrestrial relationships.

4. Outside: Nothing

The imposing cathedral of Chartres has a heavy heart and inspires respect. On its façades a green mould absorbs the humidity of baroque gone wild, evoking in its nooks and crannies a return to terror via arrogant grimaces. On the ornamental moulding of the great central arch there is a glorious panoply of 24 joyous old men, each one bearing a musical instrument. They symbolize our ancestors having attained the state of human consciousness.

In the centre stands the majestic Christ who dominates the earth currents beneath his feet. We come back to the same allegories as at Chartres.

Sanctuaries on the route leading to Santiago de Compostela have very often been placed on Celtic foundations. Worship took place, originally, in a sacred place in the forest. The tree, whose roots plunge into the earth and whose top touches the sky, was the intermediary between man and the divinity.

Compostela remains that green and humid tree. Nowadays the four points of the cathedral must distressfully serve as antennae for the transmitter that stands on a hill four miles from the city. We may laugh about the recent erection of a power television transmitter with its gigantic antenna, for on the same site, just a few metres away, clasped in the claws of modern technology, we find a large stela from ancient times. It has the form of a menhir, and its subtle emitting face is aimed south-eastward at the principal façade of the cathedral. (Tapping cosmic rays from the south-east is a technique frequently used, as pointed out several times in earlier chapters.)

Was it really necessary that modern engineering be installed right beside a site especially propitious for ancient transmissions?

It would seem that this hill was predestined to *télédiffusion* in all its aspects.

The stela is composed of the same granite as the sanctuary of Compostela. Four subterranean streams intersect underneath the transmitter stone, supplemented by four lines of the Hartmann network, forming an accumulation of crossings with diagonal telluric lines. Placing the biometer in front of the south-east face, under an encrusted cross, gives us the astonishing vibration of 18,000 units. Did this stela already have as its *raison d'être* to amplify the existing vibration of the site and so to reinforce the "miracle" effect so much expected of Santiago de Compostela?

Now it is the powerful transmitter which has the upper hand and which plays with its cathode-ray tubes so as to reach the little screen and condition the collective mentality.

CHAPTER 8

Pilgrimage Destinations

1. Variations on a Theme

Pilgrimage destinations all have water as the element in common; this blood of the earth has an influence on the surface. It can transform the oscillating circuit of the site and, according to a German researcher, works to modify the electric and magnetic potential of our blood cells.

These begin to resonate with the frequency of the spot. Microwaves on a watercourse have a higher electrochemical potential at the edges of the stream. A reduction in the radiation of thermic neutrons will be noted there. This has already been mentioned in our introduction to geobiology.

It seems to have been possible to reconstitute the original special qualities in locations where religious edifices have been built above Celtic places of worship. There is a nearly euphoric atmosphere, doubtless the same that the Celtic priests, the Druids, attempted to establish.

Measuring the effect of microwave radiations from the endocrine glands makes it clear that we enter the psychosomatic domain. Characteristically there is a considerable acceleration of the thymus gland's activity, having in its turn an influence on the health or mood of the individual.

The person who decides to make a pilgrimage is often one who suddenly feels like a stranger in the environment where he must keep body and soul together, where he begins to feel as if he is simply passing through. His daydreams are rather sentimental, and perhaps he desires unconsciously to go to a specific place in order to try to identify with He who blessed the site. He may seek to somehow substitute himself for the master chosen according to his religious beliefs. These are obscure, deeply affecting sufferings; partial success is as difficult to support as partial misery.

Once at the pilgrimage site, if he does not succeed in feeling that longed-for, subtle and bewitching insight, he will at least have been caught for a moment in a sustained vibration that will provide a small reward and the feeling of having absorbed a part of an evident force transcending self.

He will uncontestably have felt an urge toward therapeutic action, to try to draw on a powerful but indistinct regenerator or transformer, so as to graft that voltage to his personal life current.

Will he then know how to transmute these unconscious energies? . . . that is the question. Will he know how to put in a fresh fuse, that little nothing which permits a dynamic return to the light?

On the other hand, do not forget there are risks in seeking identification, without speaking of overdoing it. Man should not forget his role as an incarnated being. Even if he should be lucky in moving between the different thresholds of consciousness, he can only pass judgement on himself at the level of human discernment.

Whether his pilgrimage be only a day of escape from banality or the joy of transcendence, the experience of that fleeting instant arouses tremendous hope.

Remember Aristotle, who sought to create a rapid, violent emotional shock, so as to relieve the patient and liberate him from the pathogenic influence, until then repressed in the deepest part of his being.

It is as effective as a pharmaceutical drug of high quality.

Lourdes
Lourdes is an outstanding pilgrimage destination which raises the troubling question of miracle cures, considering there are so few chosen, so few successes. He who supports badly his bodily ills is obliged to ask why his neighbour is so much better after the pilgrimage – and why not himself? You have to have participated in one of those great nocturnal processions, to have been overwhelmed by the tragic spectacle of thousands of handicapped people in wheelchairs who, with as many candles lighting the night, proclaim their faith with emotional intensity. It would seem to take little for those powerful *Aves*, repeated over and over again, to pierce to the heavens – without unsettling the gods.

It appears that he who suffers only from psychomatic troubles will profit from these solemn moments. But for the immense mass of these human bodies the waters of Lourdes are too heavy, the slabs of a reinforced-concrete cathedral make a shelter that is too ponderous.

This being, after a brief day of hope where he felt better, will go home to his solitary armchair and, when melancholy comes again, will slip back into his inner disintegration. It is likely that his assigned role of sick person will require that he go back to the same place as before. And there, how many are they who neither know nor want to know that the precise spot where they stay can play a primary role? We are not joking: these people are perhaps permanently situated on a geopathogenic point. They are going to dive right back into the same stationary state which will only get worse.

In life's merry-go-round no one escapes from a moment of discouragement: let him remind himself of a place where once he was given the feeling of inner peace. This vivid recollection may be like a wave of life and a recharge of energy that will permit him to renew his appointment with existence.

2. Miracles à la Carte

The living water of a power point may not be enlivening at just any hour of the day or night.

The knowledge of chronobiology is one of the most important factors, but how many of us seem determined to ignore it?

A medicament, especially a homoeopathic medicine, can be beneficial in a given quantity at a given time of day, while the same dosage taken at an unfavourable time can either have no effect at all or even provoke a negative reaction.

For miracle baths, by analogy, it is essential and imperative to choose the moment of contact with the water in a sacred place. The ignoramus sets out on his pilgrimage like buying a lottery ticket, hoping ardently that he will have drawn a lucky number . . .

To follow a standard itinerary according to rudimentary, material criteria is simply going ahead blindly. Contact with that other resonance which puts everything back into order, physically as well as psychically, cannot be just a game of chance.

Nevertheless, on this road everyone has a right to breathe the Light.

Man must relearn the rhythms of life, of the seasons, of constructive hours. For anything that he wants to consolidate he should use, among other indications, the period of the waxing moon, and he should choose the cycle of the waning moon for his purification. There should be no question of going, with open clumsiness, against the current.

Visions

With our eyes turned toward heaven in a poetic and euphoric universe, all the while keeping our feet on the ground, let us concede that indefinable structures can form sporadically above ground embracing condensed radiation. Such defies all accepted laws and can make a strong impression on sensitive people. These locations are always found in relation to the meandering of underground streams influencing the human vegetative system. The pious soul will see in these nebulous formations a shape or a vision, which will lead him to proclaim a miracle.

Such places often being the ancient site of Celtic worship, in whose ground a ferromagnetic circle is buried, it is easy enough to locate it with precision.

As for analysing this formation of mist, a difference of ionization can only be measured at a certain distance above the ground. Measuring too near to the terrestrial surface shows no significant difference.

Besides, it has been proved that the stronger the terrestrial magnetism, the colder it will be on the ground.

This phenomenon of visions can also account for the magnificent spectacle of the Fata Morgana, when an atmosphere saturated with light and dark vapours can make the figures of men and horses appear above the Mediterranean off Calabria. This kind of exalting vision can flow like nectar through our misty thinking.

All of this is in relation to large surfaces. The visionary will have seen and believed everything in his own little private universe. The perfume of mystery always lingers in the unexplainable, and yet in certain cases the current will have passed.

3. Where Corpses remain Intact

Another type of cosmo-telluric power point are the sepul-
chres of religious personalities whose physical remains do
not deteriorate, even after decades or centuries (without
mummification). Such persons have chosen the sites of
their tombs themselves, during their lifetimes. At present
about sixty such cases are known throughout the world.

Let us mention a case that we have been able to study
closely, one which combines the aspects typically observed
so far. This is the case of Charbel Makhlouf, a Maronite
monk whose corpse has remained intact since 1898. His
guardians change his clothing, which shows perspiration
stains, every two months. You can find him at Annaya in
Lebanon.

The case of this personage is interesting from three points
of view:

1. he is one of those who designated himself the precise
   spot where his corpse should rest after death;
2. the interior of the convent is neutral, free of the
   Hartmann network, for a distance of 10 metres (33
   feet) around his tomb. A zone of condensed H rays
   forms an invisible barrier outside the convent walls.
   One can almost make this into a rule if one is willing to
   go to the trouble of making these numerous reproducible findings!
3. lights resembling blazing sunlight appeared above his
   tomb several months after his interment; they remained visible at long distance for 45 nights. The
   numerous witnesses to the phenomenon are trust-
   worthy: there are written statements from Sheik
   Mahmoud Hémadé, prefect of the province, from
   high officials of the convent and from numerous
   priests.
   There exist photographs of other places showing
   similar visions of luminous red balls. It may be asked
   if a parallel should not be drawn with the blazing
   lights seen in Lebanon. If the facts are true, we would
   be wrong to cast doubt on these photographs by
   hinting that they could have been faked.

In a general way, these undeteriorated corpses on sites
with high vibrations remain intact so long as they are not

displaced. Those bodies which have been disrespectfully shifted from one place to another have immediately disintegrated into dust.

Ancient Egypt has given us a picture of the funerary itinerary, ensuing from a scientific revelation applied to the practice of embalming. Here it is different: there has been no calling on special procedures; the relationship between earth and body has kept its secret.

Certain hypotheses prefer to attribute the intact preservation of a physical body after death to a musical chord which the deceased would have composed while still alive, with a view to maintaining a certain materialized vibratory form during a determined period. In sum, this would be a projection aimed toward the future, so as to remain an observer of his own mutation.

Quite a programme.

During their lifetimes these personages, having access to this vibratory world, would often harmonize their names to the frequency of the numbers and letters which compose them. We rediscover this power only in the ancient languages and the sacred languages, for our contemporary idioms are empty of this creative force. Today's numerology is often employed with a great deal of fancy, but it can serve as an amusing game.

There are certainly cases where people have bloomed after having changed a given name which was instinctively not agreeable. There we are on different terrain, ensuing from sound vibrations.

What is worrying about the undergrowth of today's vibratory fields is the incorrect utilization of electronic techniques. It is most dangerous to have awakened this lion; all of man's laws risk being powerless to control the deplorable experiments being done by too many apprentice sorcerers. One opens the way and the whole pack surges through.

Within these systems of vibratory games there remains the enigma of corpses preserved intact on a selected site.

4. Fictitious Power Points
There is no lack of *so-called* power points, in fact fictitious; the unexpected approach to geobiology risks separating the true from the false.

But woe betide he who would dare to demystify such and such a site. In certain cases they are very profitable to the organizers of pilgrimages and to an entire region.

One cannot deny a certain discomfort at having been duped. The H network remains indifferent in such cases as around a so-called saint made of wax, the impulsions of the biometer are quite ordinary. When we permit ourselves to investigate the history of a place or to unearth a relevant document, it is irritating to learn from the mouth of one of the responsible people that, yes, there is effectively some doubt but it is still possible that one might find, in a sarcophagus, a bone or a fragment of the famous saint's tunic.

Nevertheless, one can be consoled in the land of pipe dreams. Around these tourist traps there are nearly always some good little restaurants that know how to brighten our lives.

CHAPTER 9

In the Field

1. Finding out for Ourselves

We are going to inspect a handful of places which coexist with the well-known "telluric serpent" on the fractured film of our terrestrial crust. There are still a lot to be discovered; everyone can taste the pleasure of doing so.

There is a deep satisfaction in finding an old church, large or small, hidden away in a secret environment, when all around us there is the grinding racket of our agitated technological world.

How to do it

In every case we have to find at least one, if not two, underground watercourses which are going to intersect very often beneath the choir of the church. If we are not trained to do that, we can simply study the condition of the walls, which may be impregnated with moss, or sniff the odour of humidity which has infiltrated and risen by capillary action. The same visible phenomenon of the presence of subterranean water can be observed on the trees surrounding the sanctuary. They will be covered with lichen or moss until high up in the branches, and the trunk will be twisted or leaning away.

Excrescences will indicate where cells have been perturbed by the edges of a stream and where, as already discussed, the microwaves have an electrochemical potential higher than in the middle of the current. There is also a certain ionization of the ground, giving off heat and measurable by infra-red rays whose intensity is restrained above the water's course.

This telluric serpent, brother of the Tibetan and Indian Naga, which is also the wivern of Chartres, is derived from the latin "vipera" or rather the Indo-European "gwer", indicating the concept of heat. To go further, this is the serpent of fire, which brings us back to the Hindu Kundalini.

Our ancestors were not only looking for sites of telluric force but they also followed closely the route of these underground veins of influence, which were symbolically represented by the snake. These pathways were declared to be sacred; they never built a home above these zones. If a wall or a hedge had to cross one, they arranged an opening for the free flow of this fluid. Man always maintained a great respect for these natural forces and he sought to integrate himself with them in a balanced relationship.

If then men avoided living above these influences of the telluric serpent, the conception of the builders was to use them for a place of worship or meditation. The effect of underground water translates itself into a subtle brake on the physical body, which favours prayer and internal activity.

In order to perceive these locations more easily we can also train ourselves to have more intuition, to sense; we must not cut our vital lines with the earth. Like the snail, let us first put out our antennae, but with discrimination. Like the exile who returns to his native land, an emotion and a vibratory link establishes itself with the place which touches most deeply one's personal history. At the same time a resonance builds up between us and the site, leading us delicately into dialogue. Today's man, too often caught in a whirlpool of anxiety and solitude, would be astonished to feel himself received into this vibratory world of which he is ignorant. He would feel a vital current of love, and in an unconscious way, it would promote in him a soothing mutation, a more alert consciousness.

These old churches are like buildings with halos, whose ages-old walls have a patina that seems to rival the paintings of the old masters. From the first it is not very difficult to feel our sympathy, our attraction to these chosen places or, on the contrary, to be aware of a hostility emanating from an aggressive or defective environment.

Here is where a little personal test applies: either we feel well and recharged, or there is an oppression and loss of vitality. The influence of a site is not always palpable but is felt by its consequences, its impact on our receptivity.

We are delighted, in a general way, that today there are dynamic tendencies seeking to discover these links with cosmo-telluric forces. Perhaps this existential attitude, which is creative and selective, is a surge of nostalgia of Being, Yin-Yang, and the need to savour what harmony exists.

2. The Coincidences are Constant

We will make an arbitrary choice and penetrate into five sites of differing conceptions, well off the main roads.

Saubion in the Landes of south-west France

This church has the discreet perfume of a violet hidden in tall grass. There is an immediate attraction for this building which cannot be explained. The two streams are there – we feel them quite strongly on the surface – and they intersect beneath the small choir.

Before the Virgin, set back beneath the first two columns, is *the* point; it makes us understand suddenly that a cosmo-telluric exchange can effectively and spontaneously redress a physical or psychic disequilibrium in humans. We quiver to know what is really there, especially when we were not expecting it.

Of course, only that which has been personally experienced can be deeply understood. We can always lend our imagination when hearing someone else tell about it, but to feel something strongly without any warning is to know that we are in touch with truth.

It is a truth which cannot be measured, which cannot be discussed; we simply understand, we know.

Morans in the South of France

Measurements made above the portico are significant: two antagonistic forces are present.

At the right when entering is found the positive influence of the cherub with a high vibration of 10,000, and at left there is a turn to the negative with the appearance of a satanic animal, which causes the vibration to fall brutally to 2000 units.

Up to this point we had not found a satisfactory explanation for this unusual way of wishing welcome at the entrance to a Christian church. But thanks to a learned priest, who understands this game, here is his thought on the matter:

A person entering this church and passing through the porch with two qualities will have himself one or other of the qualities. He will feel attracted to the side which best corresponds to his own vibration. But that also means that everyone will find his place there, for once inside he enters into unity. He will feel at ease at his level and he himself will

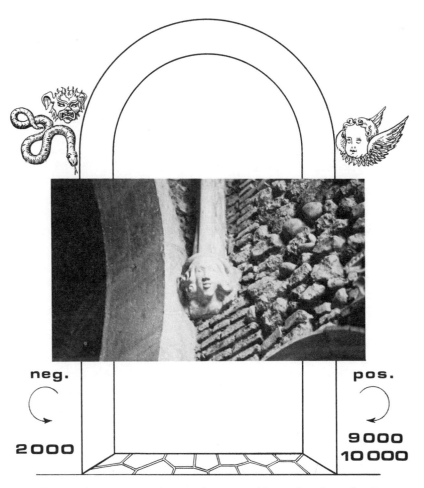

neg.

pos.

2000

9000
10000

choose always to remain on the same side, or in a lateral wing or even hidden behind a column.

Between the cherub with the high vibration and the animal there is room for all the intermediate levels; these currents are the realities of life, manifested from both sides at the top of the porch.

Does not this make for a really easy-going power point? . . . adapted to and accepting ordinary people such as they are, which is expressed at the entrance. . . .

Romainmôtier in Switzerland
Snuggled in a hollow of the French-speaking Jura mountains, this monastery dates from the year 450 and is the oldest in

Switzerland. In the seventh and eleventh centuries two churches followed one another on the same site. The last one is a marvel of Roman art, constructed by the monks of Cluny. On the inner, unobtrusive door leading to the chapel of the Virgin we find the same positive and negative figurines we found at the entrance to the church of Morans. The one on the right, the angel side, registers its 10,000 vibrations, and on the left a somewhat eroded animal faithfully maintains its low vibrations of 2000 units. Study the accompanying illustration, which concerns Morans.

The case of Romainmôtier should be emphasized, for it shows clearly that the builders of sacred edifices who applied their knowledge of the effect of underground water did not appear until between the eleventh and fourteeenth centuries.

The first two churches in this location, in the fifth and seventh centuries, were built outside the zone of water. It is only the fourteenth-century structures which had the choir placed above two streams. Here, exceptionally, they pass in diagonal lines, and, though more modestly, they are planned almost on the scheme of Chartres and Compostela.

But the intersection of these waters in that configuration must have become very disturbing and so it occurs in a spot that is less favourable, where the priest should be. For the builders it was doubtless a headache trying to reconcile an architecture pre-conditioned by the existence of two earlier churches with their own principles of integrating the underground streams. A false note crept in here, and the most difficult point behind the communion rail shows a low vibration, rarely seen in a church, of 3500 units. This point is confirmed by electronic measurements made with the oscilloscope, which registers 250 millivolts; it can be felt as an uneasiness or state of tension.

In the presbytery of the tenth and eleventh centuries, at the edge of the transept and without subterranean water, we find the noble vibration which should be found in such a place: 11,000 units, the same as in the choir at Chartres! This spot registers 70 millivolts on our oscilloscope, which is also the electrical energy requirement of our own body cells. Harmony emerges there; there is no disturbance, neither geological nor telluric.

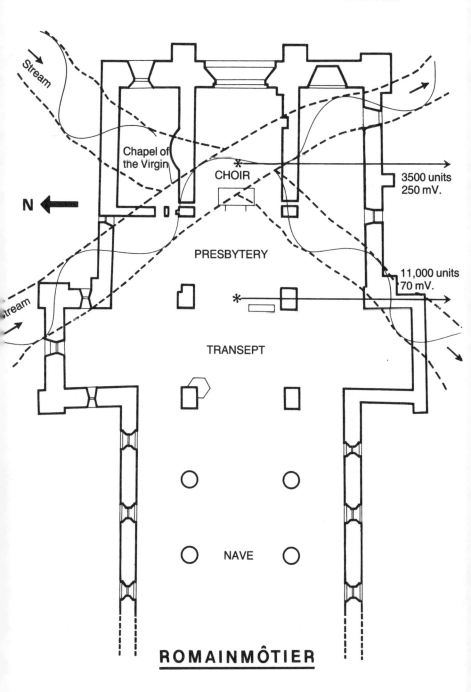

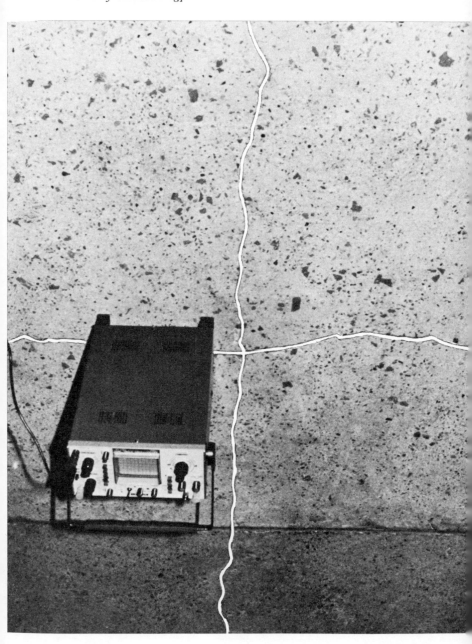

▲
Oscilloscope confirming site intensity in millivolts.

▲
Intersection of H rays corresponding to cracks in the floor.

Is Today's H Network the same as in the Eleventh Century?

There is a Hartmann knot at the north end of this presbytery, where an underground stream crosses. The lines of the H gridwork correspond exactly to the cracks in the floor, which intersect on the crossing-point. It is known that, given time, this kind of crack develops above a subterranean stream in response to microseismic activity. Even when plugged these cracks come back again in the same place.

Can we deduce that here, with a precise superposition of cracks in the floor with the H network, the telluric pattern has not changed in ten centuries?

Inasmuch as the H grid is oriented according to magnetic north and this latter moves back and forth across the ages, it is not excluded that today's Hartmann network is found on the same lines as much earlier purely by coincidence, all the while having accompanied magnetic north in its promenade . . .

Palmanova the dissident

Quite excited, we believed we had discovered a jewel of a city which, resembling a spider's web from a bird's-eye view, sticks out quite obviously as a veritable mandala.

Around the perimeter there are two fortified walls forming two nine-pointed stars, one inside the other. Clever calculation or inspiration? The Bhagavad Gita says of a bastion with nine barriers that it is the image of an initiate's body, which can close itself to infiltrations from the exterior, thus protecting the interior development.

It is an image of defence pointing to the presence of something precious and permitting access to those who know the gateways – which are nevertheless closed to intruders.

So many symbols brought together, assembled with the care of a Benedictine, invited us to measure the vibratory intensity and the telluric networks.

We are speaking of the little city of Palmanova, constructed between Venice and Trieste during the sixteenth century.

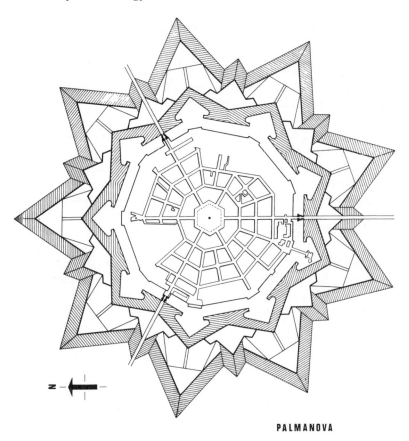

PALMANOVA

But what a disappointment! All comparable measurements fell at the most ordinary levels. In fact, the site of this city-fortress had been selected as a function of solid ground, as is said in an old manuscript. The position was favourable for protecting the Friuli region from invasion by the Turks and the Austrians.

This conception was purely military, a proud waystation on the route to the Middle East. This disappointment taught us to demystify shapes which, despite their appearance, do not have in themselves the current of initiation.

A small power point, but strong
Situated in an imposing quarry at Würenlos in the Swiss canton of Aargau, beneath a vault of nature's architecture, a

small corner of land manifests a powerful vibration comparable to the heart of the choir at Chartres.

This grotto composed of calcareous rock full of shells is like a womb, a receptacle of energy that is telluric and not at all celestial. It was discovered during the 1930s by a healer, a person herself a source of inspiration. This effervescent rock is enriched with special qualities and has even cured grave polio cases. It acts equally well on other ailments, operating in the physical sector.

This chalky rock is heavily irradiated by the tectonic structure characteristic of the site. The subterranean geography reveals that two powerful thermal streams, which supply the baths at Baden, intersect at this point.

Thus it is that quite a small surface, a spot without any worldwide reputation, can clarify and concentrate specific energies. Man will have to learn better what the genius of the earth has to offer him. The forces of nature are still too little known in our time, which, following the fad of the moment, has faith only in technology.

However the rediscovery of the elements is entirely captivating.

No guide to the power points
Is it wise to establish a tourist guide for the enthusiast who would like to recharge himself on these power points?

No, for this Emanating Force of a power point, even if it does not deteriorate over the years, risks being momentarily soaked up by the succession of crowds or even a group.

That is what can always be reported over and over again, with disappointment, at places bearing the prestigious names of

Cologne, Strasbourg, Canterbury, Florence,
Ravenna, Pisa, Milan, Rheims, Westminster . . .
and the list could be longer.

After the passing of even one lone person an energetic erosion can be remarked by measurement with an oscilloscope or a biometer; the intensity of the strong point is diminished.

It takes on average a good half-hour to re-establish the initial state of a spot, especially after it has been occupied by a person in meditation. This observation is equally valid for making these kinds of measurements on a power point.

A power point does not necessarily have to be a great church or a pilgrimage destination. The attitude of the Reform, which wanted to create an "instrument" of spiritual evolution in precise opposition to the construction of a sacred edifice, depended on the Holy Scriptures to proclaim the relative value of a sanctuary. They referred to the gospel of St. Matthew (18:20), which reads "for where two or three come together in my name, there am I with them".

Where each is in his own temple, his own guide is within him.

Establish a guide to the power points?

Honestly, is it not worth more to keep one's distance from all publicity on this subject? The joy of the discovery will reward the heart of the seeker.

3. Menhirs, Dolmens and the Hartmann Network

Derived from the Breton and Celtic languages, *Men* means stone, *Dol* means plateau and *Hir* means long.

The dolmen is a megalithic monument formed by a large flat plate laid across other vertical stones.

The menhir, by contrast, is a large tall stone planted vertically. It can be amusing to oppose the two shapes, menhir and dolmen, as two polarities, as Yin and Yang or as negative-positive.

These megaliths can be counted by the thousands

Typical dolmen.

between the Far East and Ireland, some of them weighing many tons. Their construction has been placed at 4000 years before Christ.

The dolmens, particularly those of the central Pyrenees and the Basque coast of Spain, have their major axis directed toward the south-east (again!). The effect of an interior neutral zone is reconstituted as in a power point edifice. A reproduction in miniature of three lines pushed back will be found there, surrounding the dolmen like a protective screen. The H network is repulsed in the four directions, the central zone is calm and neutral. That interior is like an absorbent silt, Yin.

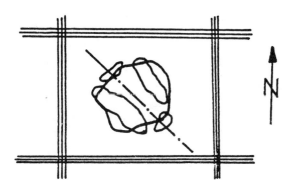

By contrast, the Yang is the menhir, and there are some which behave like real vampires. It is recognized that some people, having sojourned for more than a week in their proximity while studying them closely, have been completely devitalized. They have even needed several weeks to recover their equilibrium.

We can cite a concrete example in the Pas-de-Calais near the village of Ecoivres, where two menhirs, commonly called "the stones of Acq" but also designated the "stones of the devil", are certainly not innocent. The H network appears to be drawn to the stone, allowing itself to be deformed to marry this magnet. This is shown on the accompanying sketch in relation to the H network of the region.

The local historical society thinks these are Peulvans, monuments erected by the Celts. These stone needles are 2.55 metres and 3.10 metres (8 feet 4 inches and 10 feet 2 inches) in height, of which more than a third is buried and not visible.

Does this place have particularly evil radiations? Do the people of the countryside see the cup-like gouges as being the mark of the devils' claws?

Doubtless there have been in all epochs initiated men who knew how to find this link with the earth, the genius of the earth, and knew how to utilize its forces. Agriculture benefited from this knowledge in its beginnings. The signs which remain to us – these stone pillars – seem to have played the role of captors of energy currents, bringing greater fertility to a given perimeter.

The two menhirs of Acq or the "stones of the devil".

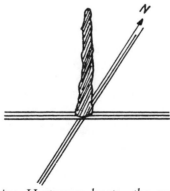

Intensified by nine Hartmann knots, the menhir becomes a transmitter.

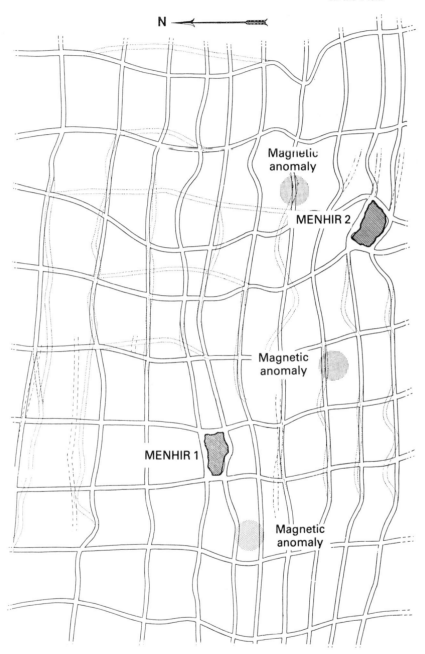

*The menhirs of Acq, called the "stones of the devil", and the H
network.*

If we take the trouble to draw these menhir sites onto a map it is noticed that they are not placed haphazardly. Generally speaking, the H network is found under a menhir in the form of three tight lines running north–south as well as from east to west, so that the menhir is intensified by standing on nine knots. Do these stones thus become captors and transmitters of energy, operating like antennae and functioning all year?

CHAPTER 10

Reserves of Subtle Energies

1. In the Future: The Tachyon Revolution

The enormous energy reserve located in Space, whose smallest particles are called tachyons, will, in time still to come, create the most spectacular of changes in the domain of alternative energy.

In the chapter on Chartres and our curious experiments made with the emission from the Virgin of the Pillar, we noted that the density of this energy field approached a billion volts per centimetre. To illustrate what this means, we could say that each human being in the whole world would be able to light his way with more than a million and a half 100-watt bulbs for his entire life.

This radiant energy is omnipresent in our universe.

This future has already begun for numerous eminent researchers; the curtain went up for the first time at congresses held in Hanover in 1980 and in Toronto in 1981. Applications in the fields of technology, economy and medicine will stimulate an indescribable shake up.

If the discovery of Wilhelm Reich was stifled for half a century, it is perhaps due to the clumsiness of a certain Mr. Einstein who in his day declared the ether to be non-existent. He recognized his error later — relatively!

In order to capture the energy of tachyons you have to force it to enter into interference with another physical system. A method might be applicable following Tesla's principle: by modifying luminous electro-magnetic rays, such as laser beams, into carrying or high frequency waves and provoking a collision with the surrounding tachyon field. Lightning functions in this way.

The study of tachyon energy is only in its infancy in the domain of orthodox physics. According to those who are knowledgeable, some surprising results lie ahead after the first teething crises. There could well be some bubbles in that great stewpot of the universe where man seeks to infiltrate his intelligence. There is a risk of burning one's fingers here and there in the beginning, as we have had the painful experience with our embryonic knowledge and first experiments, attempted by incompetent apprentice savants playing with unexplored forces.

In a future orchestrated muddle of microwaves, Evil (seeing that it does exist!) will be able to use these new channels traced by man. The struggle for domination, taking place over our heads, will make itself felt.

In parallel, another immense force of Energy is wasted, that superior form of human energy which is called, quite simply, Love. We are still too under-developed to comprehend this term.

Things begin to take shape little by little through theories that are more or less opaque. The laws of nature and the universe being, however, what they are, it is up to man to make the choice. Goethe heckled science to tell it how it should function: know how to glean knowledge from nature and know how to transmit it.

2. The Misunderstood Moon

Today we have only a feeble knowledge in the field of cosmo-telluric influences; in any event we must not forget to mention the Moon.

Our ancestors knew more about it than we do. Even if we have now set foot on the Moon, they had a real knowledge that we have too often sought to ridicule. Inasmuch as this learning was only transmitted orally, many useful aspects risk being lost with the disappearance of our grandfathers. And, nevertheless, in observing out of curiosity or in testing these stated rules we can only remain perplexed before the results, and finally we must bow before the facts.

During the five nights of full moon – the three which precede the full clarity of the moon and the two which follow – the terrestrial magnetic field is modified and has a certain influence on these "lunatic" human beings, on sleep, on births. Studies of the subject have demonstrated that the wave length of cosmic waves having a normal length of 21 centimetres (8 inches) is reduced by 50 per cent, down to 10.5 centimetres (4 inches). Modification of the oscillating circuit thus perturbs the oscillatory equilibrium of the human cell; remember that the healthy cell has a frequency of 27 megahertz (one MHz = one million vibrations per second).

What must we think, when our elders never grafted a tree during a waning moon; otherwise the tree would no longer bear fruit during a fixed number of years. Yet our present-day biological farmers apply these natural rules more and more. They plant what must bear fruit and leaves during a period of waxing moon, and they plant vegetables which must develop below ground during the waning moon.

Within the rhythm of our actions in relation to the moon everything that must be consolidated, constructed or augmented will succeed when the operations begin during a period of increasing moon and when the illuminated part of the moon is at the right (and movements toward the right will be favoured).

In contrast, everything that must be eliminated, purified or extracted will be facilitated during a period of decreasing moon, with the illuminated part of the moon at the left (and movements toward the left will be favoured). Let he who has never heard this mentioned before shake his head, but he who wants to try the experiment will be astonished and rewarded.

The moon is the life rhythm star par excellence.

That moon, although only a secondary reflection of the sun and being itself deprived of its own light, has an incredible penetrating power. The intensity of microwaves during full moon exceeds that of the sun. The penetration of lunar radiation has been reported in studies of minerals at great depth, especially by its influence on molecules and polarity. As a practical example, let us hark back to the women of the Swiss canton of Valais who used to weave their own bedsheets from unbleached linen. So that the cloth would become a dazzling white they spread the sheets on the grass during nights of full moon. If stretched out under the sun these sheets kept their original colour and even became greyish with standard washing.

Present-day information campaigns might find there some beams of light to illuminate their battles against waste and for the conservation of energy.

What is called magnetism of lunar influence is still little known. It is known that a form of magnetism which can preserve and heal is at the base of all religious rituals. The

Egyptian Book of the Dead alludes to a magnetic process through which a constant temperature is maintained inside sarcophagi. In the race toward alternative energies, to which researchers of our century will be allotted the honour of rediscovering the modalities of this principle?

Everything is nevertheless moving forward; the moon already serves as a screen for up-to-date measurements of x-rays coming from space.

And how many animals there are who hunt at night. The moon is their accomplice and reveals to them the secrets of nature, because they know how to keep them. To our eyes the moon's rays only skim over the surface of shapes, and the human hunter easily falls into traps.

Cut flowers, placed in front of a mirror during full moon, will remain open all night. They cannot follow their natural rhythm because of the photons (light particles) projected from the mirror. Do not be astonished that the human being cannot sleep because of these same reflections during full moon. If he does not want to be restless he should protect himself from the nocturnal light reflected within the room. Those flowers, in full bloom by day but also obliged to remain Beauties of the Night, will become rapidly faded at that pace. Man and woman should be able to read between the lines.

What has become of poets and dreamers since man's genius has become attracted to that crescent moon? Only the astrologer still knows how to use this planetary sign as a dimension in his horoscopes; according to his leaning he can refer to the subconscious, the imagination, or instability.

The moon herself, by her cyclic movement, will remain an indicator of the passage of time. She knows how to disappear completely only to come back again and again newly radiant; she was the only light guiding the pilgrim in the night.

Subject of innumerable myths and legends, the moon is sometimes feminine, sometimes masculine, according to the language being used.

3. Spirits Attached to a Place

It is true that within the framework of our classical geobiological appraisals made in dwellings we limit ourselves to a method of examination relevant to geological anomalies: the presence of underground water, crossing of the H network and various electromagnetic perturbations, so as to establish a diagnosis for the whole house or apartment.

However, in some specific places, it is no longer possible to ignore troubling facts which turn out to be definite phenomena. It becomes indispensable to take account of those aspects as well.

As with everything, we learn especially from experience. Even if we are incredulous, even suspicious at the outset, once we have put our finger on a latent problem, something previously unexplained – where we are confronted with a level of vibratory frequencies sharply different from the perceived world – we have to admit the evidence of an unusual, invisible presence. And sometimes there is a real menace.

The novelist easily classifies so-called haunted houses in this category, although the majority of the prisoners of this misty eternity lose themselves in the shadows. Even where the inhabitants have not yet sunk into frank neurosis, they are nevertheless distressed and are often physically de-vitalized.

In a great many of the situations which we encounter and which are repetitive, especially in houses where there has been a violent death, accident or suicide, we have been able to note the facts, almost like the antenna of a receiving apparatus which receives hertzian waves.

It truly appears that a brutal death separates the physical from the energetic body in an unharmonious way. This energetic or etheric body is, remember, a second copy of the physical body but in less dense material. When the two bodies have not been able to die at the same time, harmoniously connected one to the other, it can happen that an independent double, a sort of projection of what was the living person, lingers on the site for a certain time.

Not that these "restless souls" necessarily go around persecuting the survivors, yet confirmation is obtained that these entities or vibratory energies remain attached to a place. They feed on the vitality of the people living in these habitations. By placing an apparatus which modifies the oscillating circuit, in gigahertz frequency modulation of which the basic wave length is 21 to 22 centimetres (just over 8 inches), a prodigious change can occur: the vampire-like presence can detach itself and the inhabitants rediscover their joy of living and lose their pale and depressed aspect.

These are simple reports.

These energetic bodies, blocked without physical support in inaction, are like unfortunate fluid elements. Would we dare to allege that suicide is not a solution for escaping from our suffering, whether obvious or hidden? Would not hell be a little like that – the helplessness to withdraw one's act and thus die in peace, to say no more?

Our observations bring up another question, rather controversial: should we cremate the dead? In the Middle Ages witches and heretics were burned "so as to deprive them of resurrection and to destroy them forever". These are ancient convictions, but it is quite probable that disengagement of the spiritual body should take place slowly, progressively, in the maternal breast of the earth. Man close to primitive revelation buried his dead, which seems more in conformity to tradition than incineration.

This "protoplasm" attached to a place can take various forms, especially in the phase of mutation. In our dwellings that presence takes the shape of a flattened vibratory 8. The ∞, infinity in alchemy, also represents digestion, transformation, dissolution. In Hebrew the eighth letter signifies: water and womb, completion and abandon of life passed into rebirth.

We connect baptism with birth and rebirth. Is there a symbolic reason for constructing octagonal baptismal fonts in our sanctuaries? As a reservoir containing the substance and the essence of a creative water-energy, the baptismal font hewn in an octagonal shape serves as mediator between the square and the circle, between earth and heaven (as already mentioned). The concept of eight remains an intermediary bond of the etheric body in mutation.

These presences attached to a place have an aspect more subtle than what is said of them in the more or less frightening tales about ghosts. They are different also from certain customs in India, where one throws a stone on the road behind oneself in returning from a funeral, so as to block the spirit of the deceased in case he wanted to come back also!

Especially do not give in to fear when such cases arise; inner strength asked for and received will provide total protection. It is also preferable to avoid certain literature which proposes means of protection relying on superstition. We can cite a single ridiculous example, that of believing one is protected by sticking knitting needles around one's bed. All those points are rather subversive: it is like surrounding oneself with a forest of antennae which will greedily soak up microwaves from our modern transmitters.

This would be amplifying and muddling up the ironies of fate.

4. Malevolent Works of Art

In the domain of art we are entering a world of form and colour emissions. Objects of art, containing the expression of all the feeling or the passion of the artist, do not leave indifferent the sensitive person who captures the vibration transmitted, voluntarily or not, by the creator of the work.

The receptive individual finds a calming effect wherever harmony emanates from the lines and the colours. By contrast, he who needs a stimulant will hang on the wall a painting powered with burning red. If this kind of a composition is suspended in a child's bedroom, one should not be surprised that he will have a troubled sleep or be an overexcited little imp.

We should not hesitate to eliminate a work of art when we have become aware that it is incompatible with our deepest feelings. It exercises a secret power over the individual; in time he will no longer really be himself and he will not even be able to judge his own imprudent ignorance. The first intuition is usually the best, but we do have a tendency to listen immediately to that second wave which is grafted onto the intuition, because the second conforms more with our own secret desires.

Under the silent effect of that perfidious work of art, man continues to dance the farandole behind his mask. Matter formed by the hand of the artist often becomes the basis of a thought, whether good or poisonous. The fear of rejecting something turns the object into a tyrant.

Without dashing onto a boulevard of the imagination,

how does it happen that – and this is an actual case – the presence of a bust of oneself, placed on the bedside table, provokes insomnia, nightmares and causes a loss of strength. In front of that work of art the biometer indicates a very low vibration, less than 1000 units, a devitalizing vibration covering the materialized double of a handsome face reflecting great moral elegance. As soon as the bust was removed the physical person regained his vitality and his equilibrium.

But why was this double so greedy? Doubtless there was an influence of shape-related waves, all the more subtle because the features and contours were identical. As if two had sought to become one, the life-vibration was more and more monopolized by one at the expense of the other.

(But whoever lets himself be hooked accepts the cloying shackle.)

Beware however works of art or ancient statues which might have been used in that famous black magic: their violent influence can still have an effect, even if these objects are 4000 years old.

Such experiences can be painful, even if we do not want to believe and do not want to know anything about it. There can be a little flaw in our reasoning and then one fine day we perceive ourselves to be the naive and innocent victims of such involvements.

The real cases continue to accumulate, but there is no question here of telling sensational little stories. From the moment that we find ourselves involuntarily face to face with unknown powers, which on their side have meticulously programmed an arrogant attack, it is difficult to master them. The Koran alludes to the practices of witches, who tie magic knots on which they blow so as to bind a fate to them. Is it not strange to note that someone who is "not with it" or is attacked by a devastating entity (and admit that such exist . . .) manages to recover partial equilibrium by positioning himself on a Hartmann knot for a few moments? This is almost counter-aggression, with the complicity of the earth providing its own kind of acupuncture!

It is most important not to give in to panic, to have a confident and clear inner light, even to have compassion for this aggression; it is really difficult to use the word love, but that would doubtless be even more effective. In any seemingly absurd manifestations, often conceived in darkness and ignorance, a comprehension of that "other", a benevolent affinity can transform the worrying phenomenon. There are plenty of monumental swearwords which become inoffensive in a clever mouth.

Up to this time we have not made a dent in the inventory of all the species and variants of this weird and conceited world.

5. The Forest's Edge

Those mysterious Elementals and the world of fairy stories
This is a domain with definite signposts, but let us risk poking a stick in the anthill.

Contemplate, in the relationship of earth to heaven, how little we humans are, on one of the lower steps of the ladder of life. Yet a Multitude swirls under our feet, sometimes visible – yes! They are those energy forms situated between animal and man and called *Elementals*. At first glance we might believe ourselves falling into the most irrational of concepts, nevertheless investigators in the bio-energetic domain are more and more often digging into this unploughed field. The key to the mystery is not yet available to Mr. and Mrs. Everyman, but we are gaining perceptions through the means of:

1. observation – and by analogy on a more subtle level, through intuition;
2. listening – up to the point of clairaudience;
3. experimentation – the factual.

For a great many primitive populations – but how many are there still close to the laws of nature? – there is an innate connection with a higher consciousness, an expansion of feeling which becomes reality. However, we stand aside from talk of diabolical goblins with long noses and other weird features.

Recognize that everything is interdependent, nothing can be detached from the creative energies that cling together the length of the ladder that climbs from the knowable to the transcendent.

We are going to approach this hierarchy, invisible but

keenly vibrant, on tiptoe and disturb the *Elementals* for a moment.

So as not to only sink into the lower level, let us rapidly skim the level above man's head, the place where humanity meets those intermediaries (revealed in "La Cosmogonie d'Urantia" ★★3) under the name of *Medians*; Urantia is the cosmic name of our planet Earth. These medians, and still higher up our Adjusters of Thoughts, are linked in a network capable of guiding a simple mortal through all his ups and downs. The existence of this hierarchy does not prevent simultaneous contact, direct and immediate, with the omnipresent One.

If someone has reservations in this respect, let him keep his eyes and his ears closed until the eventual day when it will be given him to have an experience of this type. He can then reset his evolutionary clock as of his own moment of truth. May he then know how to savour it, for what is the present without the joy of awakening to a more promising tomorrow?

Speaking of that same cosmogony, it is said that within the structure of the one hundred groups of energetic wave lengths, men have already recognized sixty-four. This figure is repeated in all the new codes of scientific research: from the 64 genetic codons to the 64 mathematical grids or to the 64 vibrations of mantras . . .and other 64s.

The 64 hexagrams of the I Ching, the erudite Chinese system of transformations, complete the hypothesis: we will have taken a giant step when the 64 entities of our intimate personal environment will have made themselves known.

The universe of fairy tales
It is really a puzzle for the conscience to know whether, in this chapter on subtle and unknown energies, it is permissible to make a slight digression into a certain aspect of fairy stories and the world of *Elementals*. Integrating the subject in this discussion responds to the wishes of researchers who have also discovered the existence of this little-explored domain. These well-known professors have promised to come out of the shadows the day of their retirement; until then they prefer to avoid the condescending smiles of their

colleagues and they seek especially not to irritate the sources of grants.

The demarcation between man and *Elemental* is indistinct. A first trigger for us was to meet a paralysed person, in a wheelchair, who knew how to make use of these *Elementals*, invisible to our eyes, as the kind of domestic helpers that one might meet in a story. This person, of healthy spirit and perfectly balanced, even erudite, directed us toward an astonishing but possible technique of access. Recovered from our stupefaction, it proved to be our first perception of the stakes in a reality still veiled.

In an incoherent universe these *Elementals* or energy forms are partially endowed with superior intelligence, nevertheless being without their own will power they yield to the orders of man. They are called "djinn" in Arabian; they are no secret to the students and the sons of the medicine men called marabouts.

These *Elementals* live in an autonomous fashion and in other conditions than the human community. Although they are often manageable and good-natured, they are sometimes unsociable – we cannot predict their immediate reactions. These entities live in our personal environment, but it is up to us to take the first step in meeting them. Otherwise they will continue to circulate around us with total indifference and without our being aware of them.

Even if we cannot fully interpret this parapsychological concept, that does not justify immediately questioning the probability. Only the experimentation that we accomplish ourselves is capable of lifting us above these sterile doubts.

Is this world of fairy tales of a purely subjective order? We enter into the following dialogue:

A. "You who are lucky enough to have that transcendental faculty, you who have that way of looking which experiences a reality often inaccessible to most mortals – tell us!"

B. "With only our limited human vocabulary, would it not be better to remain silent?"

A. "Why not share it with us? There is an extraphysical, present world which is revealed to you, and we want so much to hear about it from you, because at first you were the incredulous one, who now approaches these new realities with a scientific spirit."

B. "All these phenomena trouble us because we passed quickly through a window of unexpected revelations, but we still have our old conception of things. It is an eternal theatre of contradictions."

A. "We will be like very good children who want to hear a strange but true story."

B. "The essence of fairy tales must flow in the veins of the writers who relate these stories and they themselves have surely been able to have this kind of experience. These impressions, starting as pure sensitivity, can take shape. These beings have the faculty of slowing down their own fast vibration so as to adopt a more or less materialized form."

A. "Inasmuch as we have not experienced it personally, we will not continue to be stubborn; but it is worth the trouble to hear you and, it is a promise, we will poke fun at nothing without examination."

B. "We must not clumsily do violence to the character of things but try to comprehend the combinations of dynamism that nature puts into play. It is not a question of unleasing forces that later you will no longer know how to dominate."

A. "The desire for verification is not simple curiosity but an attempt to reinforce our base of knowledge."

B. "If you admit that the complex human being is a microcosm patterned after the macrocosm, the universe, then you can understand that these hypersensitive creatures, gifted with clear-sightedness, can take in manifestations of astral forces, which seem supernatural at first contact. These phenomena are like variable vibrations, making an impression on our physical and etheric organs (the latter being the chakras) and transmitted to the human "Naos" or brain. While this notion is as old as the world, certain of our contemporary researchers are commencing, and not without astonishment, to find that the Ancients were sometimes right!

The animals are without doubt a great deal more sensitive than humans and they sense more easily the presence of invisible entities. The dog and the horse, in particular, will suddenly show fright although the man neither sees nor senses anything. The cat, in contrast, will purr happily when meeting this same charged current. Note that in geobiology numerous observations made on cats confirm that they like to stay on crossing points of the H network. These knots are particularly geopathogenic points for the human being, the dog and the horse.

The cat who comes around rubbing against our legs discharges us of an accumulation of static electricity; he is a real miniature lightning rod."

A. "Each being is a carrier of different electric and magnetic forces which play a non-negligible role on earth and in the cosmos. One of the practical applications of these forces is the laying-on of hands through which pass the human magnetic fluid, for good or for evil. How can we become conscious of this play of forces which slumbers within us?"

B. "The profound self, or if you prefer, the subconscious in which is written the lesser movements of the soul – the soul which breathes life – coordinates the impulse of natural forces. Man, belonging simultaneously to the physical level and the spiritual level, is capable – through a perfectly natural law – of capturing certain signals from another dimension."

A. "When dialogue with a Presence – whether incarnate or not – is established in our thoughts, is there not a modification of our own being at the moment this occurs? We are no longer completely ourselves, there is a kind of sharing and exchange of our reciprocal energies."

B. "Yes, the georhythmogram indicates it clearly: when we measure someone's cutaneous resistance, alone in his room, from the moment when a second person enters the room the curve in kOhms rockets upward; it even happens in blindfold tests, that is to say, when the individual being tested has eyes and ears covered and does not know what is taking place.

The individual will be even more moved to fragment himself by the presence of three or several people."

A. "Individuals alone, also certain children, sometimes have the habit of being in dialogue, perfectly naturally, with the Presence of their choice, often not noticing that they are speaking aloud. Evidently, if they are in a conventional setting, that can take a turn for the worse; with our pretensions of being disciplined and well-balanced, we quickly classify them as unhinged and lost in the world of make-believe."

Approaching the Elemental

A. "Tell me now what you have learned of these other dimensions, on the ladder of hierarchies. You place man between the two universes, one of them immediately above him, the other at an intermediate level between man and animal which you call the *Elemental*. Does it really exist?"

B. "Two questions, of broad scope and at the same time of extreme simplicity, to be inserted into the great wheel of natural laws. Before slipping into the world of the *Elementals*, I want to remind you of the upper level, which is better known. It is man's possibility of contact with the beings of Light. For some people these are angels, dislncarnate masters, spiritual guides, synthesizing powers, purification and illumination.

I have already referred to the Medians, in the sense of the cosmogony of Urantia, according to which these are immortal beings who can communicate with men in certain circumstances but who are normally invisible to them. The Medians dispose of a system of archives or memories, witness of everything that has happened on Earth since the beginning of its existence – a system which is infinitely more rapid and more perfect than the electronic memories of our modern computers.

One Median in four can be rendered visible to the human eye under certain conditions; even in their invisible form the Medians can act on matter as messengers or protectors. This is a marvellous doctrine of interdependence, of conscious ties and of energy transmission. The dialogue can be a kind of prayer of divine essence, linked to the living God. That instrument above our heads is not at all heavy; on the contrary, if well-tuned it can sing and often does not lack a sense of humour!"

A. "There is man stuck on his planet between these ethereal energetic forms on the one hand, and that other world, the *Elementals* over which the average person exercises no conscious control. Is it there that fairy tales can take root? Along with dwarfs, nymphs, elves and other spirits?

Is there not a hidden sense in these stories and legends?"

B. "I have learned more of the earth than about men; what men think is often only truth for them alone. Besides, among all the names in this subhuman kingdom there is 'gnome', which comes from the Greek 'gnosis' and means Knowledge.

This intermediate world lives in nature. Some places are more favoured than others. Let us guide and instruct, for where it is possible to observe these forces of nature in absolute silence, they take shape little by little. The vibrations we pick up will create forms bit by bit, in the same way that the Creation was unleashed by the vibratory power of the Word, and with some luck and a good frame of mind we will see the light of discovery.

Among the Ancients the forests were consecrated to the divinities; there is the mysterious dwelling of the spirit of place. The undergrowth remains a centre of life for the *Elementals*; with its high grass it is an inexhaustible reservoir of knowledge where our own meagre grasp of natural science seems too schoolbookish. In numerous regions of Asia the trees, the forest, are the residence of local genies – as it is with us – and the relationship with the *Elementals* is on the land rather than in the sky.

The forest only opens its Bible a crack for those who know how to read.

Lakes are revered as subterranean palaces, from which fairies, nymphs, and mermaids spring up. The lake is sometimes also considered to be the eye of the earth or the mirror through which the *Elementals* can observe man, animals and plants."

A. "And what are these energies, who are unknown to most men? Tell us how these *Elementals* show themselves and what you know of them. We have to overturn the total of our abilities and sharpen our perception so as to disentangle and penetrate these subjects that we do not know much about."

B. "There is an underlying impetus of great energies, several of which are linked to the curative quality of . . . Love. Nature only unveils her secrets to those beings who are respectful of that over-nature, who know how to avoid making a bad joke of it. For in this world of *Elementals* there exists a complete spectrum of characters, copied after humans (!), with which they impregnate themselves and who they imitate with a great deal of clumsiness.

It seems to be confirmed that these *Elementals* do not have their own willpower. Thus they will submit to the orders of a human being. Man will be disconcerted in his routine if, even under his leadership, the *Elementals* do not exhibit very high qualities. However, there are also some who are real helpers and collaborators; you must never fail to thank them, so that good relations – intelligent and natural but often seeming rather mysterious – will be durable.

It is always risky to venture into an unknown world, but it is not necessary to involve oneself with everything. It is indispensable to make a choice among the *Elementals* who should serve or who are to be discovered.

Overdiversification is always devitalizing.

Instead of moving through a fog of aberrations, it is better to commence simply by sitting down against a tree-generator, a healthy oak for example, and feel the subtle strength which it gives us. Relax – the lake only reflects the sky when it is calm."

A. "What are the groups and varieties of *Elementals* mentioned in fairy tales? Do the known symbols correspond to your observations?"

B. "You are right to talk about groups. When I really think about it, they are nearly always several, in a clan. They are timid at first; I am going to tell you a personal experience about discovering water sprites."

A. "I cannot wait to know all about your discovery. In Nordic legends they were identified with nymphs and were gifted with a certain clairaudience. Flirtatious, mischievous and sometimes cruel, they took pleasure in enticing man to the bottom of the water where he died, exhausted, in their arms; magic spells through water and love.

I would like to meet these water sprites once myself –
how did you do it?"

A true fairy tale

B. "There are unforeseen encounters that happen by
chance along the way, but it is better to prepare a precise
plan of approach.

One time I had the luck, without believing it too
much, to sense some vibrations becoming even more
dense in a clearing. After an hour of silent waiting
hidden in some high ferns, it was given to me to see the
shapes of my first *Elementals* emerge as if from a fine
spider's web and take form before my eyes. The general
impression was as if a large eye was observing me,
questioning me. But I was still doubtful of myself,
telling myself that perhaps it was only my imagination.

Several years passed, the nuances of the vibratory
energies surrounding beings and things began to
become clear; to me they appeared to be an integral part
of the natural laws.

It is a matter of blending what you know with what
you feel.

Coming back to the world of water sprites, I began
by determining the place where they ought to be found
through remote divining on a topographic map. I fell
upon a marshy, uninhabited zone about twenty yards
from the water's edge in the upper reaches of Lake
Léman.

To assure that my observations would be as objective
as possible, I did not want, in case of success, to be the
only witness. So I asked a friend, a medium in his spare
time, to accompany me late one autumnal afternoon.

We left the car at a respectful distance and walked
toward the site without saying a word or making other
noise. There, about three or four yards apart, seated on
dry leaves, we no longer moved, nor coughed, nor
sneezed – observing complete immobility for more than
two hours, identifying ourselves with the trees and the
high grass. Keeping relatively still for such a long time is
really believing, almost an act of faith.

We were rewarded, for suddenly a breath of warm air
began to swirl around us. About ten yards in front of us

we distinguished, between the trees, a pale glow, opaque and phosphorescent. At the same time the birds set up the kind of din with which they warn of an intruder.

Our eyes never left this formation, which gained in strength and intensity, taking the shape of a giant dull green egg. Once again we had that paralysing impression of a great eye observing us intensely.

There we were face to face with that strange form of life, mutually scrutinizing one another. By a movement of his eyebrows my friend signalled me that something was happening . . . a first step in assuring me that I was not victim of a hallucination.

We sought a way to establish a climate of confidence through mental accord, adopting a higher thought vibration, a kind of transmission offering sympathy and security – a specialist would speak of emitting alpha waves.

The opaque patch began slowly to lighten as a fog dissipates. Then it was almost the stage of a theatre on which there appeared a parade of lithe feminine shapes, in a mysterious moss-green light. Very slowly they advanced in our direction, huddled up close against one another, slipping prudently forward, clearly with great fear but propelled by a certain curiosity. They stared at us like fearful, inquisitive little animals, advancing then withdrawing a little, then each time coming farther forward.

Before these slender shapes of an exquisite delicacy, whose still formless faces took on the same radiation as the great eye which had preceded them like a scout, I felt a kind of luminous projection settle on my face, something which resembled a chill dew freshly deposited.

Wondering if I had not surrendered to a daydream, I noted the enthusiasm of my companion who, by a flick of his eyelids, once again confirmed that he too saw what was unfolding before us in an incredible fashion.

With still more patience these delicate sisters came closer to us. They seemed to listen to the leaves talking.

Like a watermark on paper, everything about them had that soft greenish cast, and I was reminded of a

Scandinavian legend which says that water sprites have dull blue-green hair which they comb coquettishly just at the water's surface.

It had to happen: by an unpardonable and involuntary gesture, I put a brutal end to this unique spectacle because a little beetle stung me. Instantly, with my movement, this marvellous picture dissipated. Everything had been prepared and woven with such patience, like an incomparable spider's web; it only needed a rotten stroke of the scissors in one of those threads to make this marvellous vibratory song collapse. Night fell on our disappointment; everything was wiped out as if a roaring rainstorm had washed earth and heaven. Trees oozed a few tears of sap; we and the grass were chilled with humidity.

We found ourselves plunged back into a reality where, however, nothing had changed. But yes! The birds suddenly resumed singing at full volume. In fact, while these visions lasted, they had remained silent, camouflaged, as if a big cat was wandering in the vicinity. And in us there was exhilaration tinged with a sob!

On the way home, discussing and matching up our observations, which proved to be identical, we could at least deduct that this world of *Elementals* did indeed exist. And, perhaps, one day a laser beam might be adapted to clarify these facts, in the sense that LASER = Light Amplification Stimulated by Emission of Radiation.

Looking at my companion, who was more than fifty years old, I asked myself with surprise what had happened to him. It was quite striking: he seemed suddenly to be a lad of perhaps twelve years of age. I said nothing about it.

But the next morning on the telephone, at the end of our conversation, he said: 'You know, last night, I did not dare tell you, but you looked to be between fifteen and twenty years old'. This had to be verified in the mirror! To my stupefaction, there really were no wrinkles. I looked like a green apple not yet ripe, and that exceptional state continued for three days!

Those dear little water sprites caused us to pass

through the most mysterious and extraordinary salon of fleeting rejuvenation; we had entered deeply into an ageless world.

Now there is a fairy tale, a real one!

Without being misunderstood, would it be happier to choose objectively and coldly to live without ever fishing for such tender images?"

A. "What can be said of those other *Elementals* who skipped through our childhood picture books?"

B. "Through enchantment we risk not distinguishing the false from the true. Geniuses are considered models for various collective groups, such as armies or professions. There are good *Elementals* and perverse geniuses, well-trained servants faithful as a dog, but do not identify them with dark forces if it is only a matter of vibrations at ground level, slower, heavier.

We attribute to elves, fairies and nymphs a freshwater environment. As for those famous photos of fairies that have been circulating for more than half a century, allegedly authenticated by Sir A. Conan Doyle – how many of our contemporaries have openly admired them! – it took the recent revelation of he who made the photo to prove that public opinion had been hoaxed for 75 years.

Nevertheless, I offer thanks to our *ondines* for having sculpted a fine smile of light on the narrow mask of my face!"

6. Reserves of Subtle Energies

(a) Two great energies

There will always be a fragment of the Inexplicable, and it will remain silent.

It is also a temptation to approach supersensitive reality. A greater willingness to accept the facts would permit establishing a hypothesis, which would incite the seeker of truth to go further. Sometimes the dust falls away from our eyes by itself, but man, a prisoner of fear facing the unknown, will often take refuge in the easy way or take the side of professional dissidents, who are compelled to reject everything that is not expressed in a certain jargon.

Everyone is free to breathe under the leaden skies of his prejudices.

It is desirable that information derived from living science not be reserved uniquely to an elite. Each of us knows how to recognize and appreciate the taste of salt.

The great reservoir of Space, seemingly inexhaustible, containing the most subtle of energies, is destined to open a fascinating future to us. Let us refer back to the beginning of this chapter which skims over the era of tachyons. In parallel with what future technology will realize with its computerised brain, a new race of thinkers will doubtless come to the fore, either simultaneously or at a regular rhythm. There is a vibratory understanding of high quality in that universal Substance which produces everything.

In our humanity there are some chosen men–antennae who receive a continuous signal emitted by mediators or medians. Where there is synchronization is where the Love vibration can be born. And that is the second or greatest of the energies.

Which is what the whole world is waiting for!

Impartial research is motivated by these two inexhaustible reserves. A world thirsty for the "green" dawn seeks to achieve a new climate, but we must acknowledge that for the moment we are suffering birth pangs. Man's evolution will be to adapt himself to. shifting forms and not to imprison himself in prideful prejudices.

(b) What the flower does

Humanity's neat little preoccupation, on this earth which gives and takes away life, is to know how to regenerate himself and to be in harmony with his personal micro-climate.

How does one develop oneself in this subtle world and how does one use that cosmo-telluric breath, which lies outside profit-and-loss statements? Will it be a windfall or a misfortune when the economists also discover that there is profitable energy to be exploited? Without remaining frozen in the red ink of ambiguity, seekers and their researchers will have to find a good balance between the subjective and the objective.

We can only rejoice in such an opening; it is a marvellous and formidable adventure through fascinating fields.

But watch out: even as true love is always threatened, in this new state of sensitivity the hard blows will also be felt in a more violent way.

To be open on one side and know how to protect the other – there is a strategic challenge!

Are we not ourselves, through our own cells, real power stations of natural energy? Each cell is a miniature radio receiver with its own wave length of about 22 centimetres (8⅔ inches). The cell needs electric energy in order to receive the transmission; where will it find those 70 millivolts? It must come from the cell's own liquid, 97 per cent of its composition at the moment of formation. The human of 60 or 70 years still has 60 to 65 per cent fluid in his cells.

The well-balanced cell has, remember, a frequency of 27 megahertz. It will receive this fundamental energy in the form of emissions or waves coming from nature and the earth. What does a flower tell us when its measurements are compared with ours? Remember the method of the biometer which is based, according to the physicist Bovis, on the unit of measure called the angstrom (A°), the unit of length employed in microphysics. Let us recall that one A° = ten millionths of a millimetre. The colour red corresponds to 6500 A°, which is adopted within the framework of large, precise structures. Taking a beautiful red tulip, for example, we actually get 6500 units.

Let us simply observe this flower: when a sunbeam shines on its petals and produces a luminous transparence, the vitality of this same tulip rises to as much as 7200 units. In normal lighting it regains its basic vibration.

Thus the contribution of photons – light particles – is indispensable and augments the vitality of everything that lives. These states of shifting between shadow and light also have an influence on our psychic behaviour.

The flower gives off its most exquisite perfume at the most beautiful moment of its life. There is a beautiful Hindu legend which says that at the moment of blossoming out the flower gives us its soul. Who dares to bluster that these are only superficial observations and that it is all nothing but froth?

Let us concentrate on observing the ageing of a jonquil of the genus narcissus, which has six white petals and an orange interior disc.

The faded white petals have a vibration of no more than 1200 units, which corresponds to a state of great decline but still attached to a thread of life. By contrast, the orange centre maintains intact for a very long time its energy of 6700 units, despite the aspect of a faded flower.

That strongly resembles our own external ageing, faded and wrinkled, transparent through loss of energy and vitality.

But the sun centre, our solar plexus, holds on like that flower, fervent until the end. At the same time, our warm and luminous interior has the ability to prolong within us an intense life-vibration, for the wrinkled skin is the periphery which often only sees itself in others.

However, the external aspect loses its importance in vanity, when the weight of true values has been displaced. The intact centre is an energy-consciousness beyond all norms; it regenerates itself in silence.

(c) Silence in the south-east

Silence is a ceremony in monastic rules; it is always a launching pad for a new surge. According to tradition there was a Silence before the Creation.

The energy contained in the silence of dawn, when the heavenly vault re-emerges still empty of colours, is rich in vital potential, in dynamic recharging.

From the moment of first light, when change occurs progressively, birds set up a great chattering and melodious flights of song. He who observes carefully will note that, five minutes before the sun appears, our feathered friends become silent again. It is a solemn moment when energy seems to be condensed to a maximum, and when one concentrates, one does not chatter.

What if man also were to go silent during those few minutes?

Man can benefit from that supply of vital energy by positioning his head at the east, in his work or in his nocturnal recuperation. This will be translated into greater strength and physical resistance. It is easy enough to demonstrate with a simple energy receiver conceived by – hold on – the Ancient Egyptians. By directing that energy to the level of the "Tu Mo" meridian (on certain points the length of the spinal column) the weakened person will feel recharged and fortified. This is quite useful when the Yang has separated from the Yin, when energy is separated from matter.

On the other hand, the ancient Chinese had a construction law which required that dwellings be oriented within the terrestrial magnetic field, with the effect that people slept with their heads at the north. It can be confirmed today, in effect, that when the blood cells are in harmony with north-south bipolarity they show a more fluid current of energy. Practically speaking, this assures a more refreshing sleep due to an influence on the microstructure of the cytoplasm.

South-east
It is astonishing to note during our investigations at all latitudes that the principal façades of sacred edifices are oriented to the south-east. Innumerable observations made with a contemporary instrument, containing minerals and crystals and designed to correct a perturbed environment, demonstrate that cosmic radiation coming from the south-east best re-establishes troubled equilibrium. The American physicist Kenneth Emerson has written a study on the power of certain stones and crystals having specific molecular textures and specific vibratory rates, to act not only on the environment but on subtle bodies as well.

We have already cited the similar orientation of monolithic monuments having the role of transmitters directed toward a sanctuary and which always point to the south-east. This makes a happy marriage: the east with its vital force and the south with its fire and its sun, the most antique of energies yet simultaneously the most up-to-date. The south-east still has much to reveal to us; for the moment it prefers discretion.

(d) Brandy at the tea party
Water is a nearly free gift of nature, a flood of energies; it is not only that fine chemical formula, it is not only H_2O.

Under all the forms that we can imagine – from the clear brook to rivers and lakes, rainwater under the sun's rays giving us a marvellous gamut of colours, from the quiet water of a small lake to the most prosaic of household taps –

its action is to serve man and everything that lives. Some avant-garde experiments have shown that water is the carrier of vital energy and constructive forces. At the technical level these demonstrations would be of the highest importance for the problems now appearing which concern our drinking water. We discover that a water, even purified, chemically and biologically beyond reproach, lacks vitality! It is dead water from this point of view, and it is not necessary to insist on what an element without life can contribute in the way of energy, whether in the form of food or in hygienic use. What is at stake is the very existence of the future generation.

Without much restraint, certain milieux extol the energetic effect of water that has been magnetized or charged by various procedures. The enthusiastic drinker of water often sees himself disagreeably betrayed: chromatographic tests – those charts with lines that wiggle up and down – reflect, by analogy, humanity's freedom to grow or to diminish. These registrations clearly indicate the aggressive sawtooth curves of a magnetized water. We plunge too easily and too stubbornly into what we believe to be new, unlimited possibilities. Sometimes after a life of effort, with some peaks achieved, man may find himself dried out and depolarized.

More and more the individual must try to take charge of himself with care and discernment, threading through the hotchpotch of advertising and recommendations, for who better than he can judge which energy sources are best suited to him. We are loaded down with theories and dosages, but is the person who knows how to find rest and regeneration in the simplest of ways the one to be most envied? For example, burying oneself in a supple mass of sand, which adjusts womblike to his shape, gives the human a feeling of returning to the protective source. The gleam of the sea (or the snow), the complementary sparkle, is sufficient to light his way toward other passions.

We do not intend here to enter into the domain of food as an energy resource. The most important factor is making a proper source, but how often we are deceived when we want to apply a given prescription to the letter. Here again, it is a matter of not being absolute and fanatical.

There exists a method of nourishing the human body

with solar energy by photosynthesis. Does this lead in the direction of another image of man?

The other extreme would be savoury stewpots and excess at the table. What does the Sage say? We cannot resist quoting the statement of the guru Guruvakyana, who said:

"The best medicine for 90 per cent of sick men is the open air, sunshine, a beautiful girl and a good cook."

In China the spleen is considered to be a storehouse of Yin energy, earthy – an energy as versatile as shifting moods. It would thus be worthwhile to try drowning a bad mood in good humour. Laughter is a great reservoir of positive energy, as much as the perfume of society. It is said that good humour goes naturally with a high-spirited person.

How dull is the ordinary news item without a well-sharpened pencil and a humorous cartoon that relaxes and disarms. How colourless would be Paris without the poet who knows, starting from mediocre reality, how to polish and improve on fate.

To discover those subtle energies which are at hand, in the play of cosmo-telluric exchanges as well as in the colours of life, is also to know how to enjoy the quality of the present moment.

(e) Rational vs. mystical

Between rationalism and mysticism there exists a higher attitude: it is what unites them.

In each thing, in each being, form and life coexists. We will remain the frail creature who imagines himself depending on constants so long as we hold to the Catharist conception, which prefers to deprive matter of its relationship with the elusive. For the Cathar, the candle does not symbolize light; for him the wax and the wick are only matter. He does not see the support of the flame and he cannot conceive that there is a relationship, which does not prevent the materialist from passing himself off as a luminary!

Periodically the world fears a lack of all sorts of energies. There is certainly enormous waste which needs to be reprogrammed with the help of our grey matter. On the road to tomorrow, the dynamic power which sleeps in static consistency is condemned to progress but can only be invigorated by an Illumination.

A stopping point. An option for today and tomorrow: Man knowing how to master telluric currents and holding firmly to his cosmic antennae.

Symbols of ancient Siam.

We can acclaim with joy the initiative of the Sage of Princeton, whereby in 1969 hundreds of American savants affirmed that the world is surely governed by a superior force. This wise man contributed to the development of a system which incorporates all that is known into a basic logical structure so as to open toward the heights, the spirit.

That is a serious contribution to contemporary thought, a reserve of energies in the hand of springtime.

The learned person imposes on himself the discipline to not say everything. He knows that within the rational, united to a well-balanced mysticism, lies the evolution of dialogue – interior and permanent grace united to illumination without shadows.

Mental energies, adjusted to the forms of thoughts of divine essence, can then be directed toward practical goals. Everything which at first was simply a fiction then becomes a real living exchange and leads toward creating the new man, different from the old one.

Life gives and takes in the rhythm of the seasons, but personal equilibrium must be recreated anew every morning . . . the soul needs a little fresh air.

Let us know how to gather the gifts of these subtle energies, upright and fully conscious, each of us on his individual power point.

Real wealth, is it not after all a successful life?

Glossary

Adrenaline
epinephrine, an adrenal hormone used as a heart stimulant, vasoconstrictor, and a muscle relaxant.

Angstrom, Å
unit of length used in microphysics. One Å = one 10-millionth of a millimetre.

Ankh
a cross of which the upper vertical arm is a loop; a symbol of life in Egyptian iconography.

Bhagavad Gita
a poem which relates the teaching of Lord Krishna to Arjuna, the greatest archer of his time, on the battlefield; it is considered the heart and soul of the sacred Hindu text, the Mahabharata.

Biometer
ruler for measuring the intensity of a site:
2000 units on a knot of the H network;
6500 units = average physical energy;
8000 units = physical equilibrium;
11,000 units = vibration level at Chartres;
12,000 units = vibration level in a mosque;
13,500 units = etheric equilibrium;
14,000 units = vibration levels in Hindu and Buddhist temples;
18,000 units = spiritual summit of a power point.

Chakras
centres of consciousness of the etheric or energetic body; Yoga recognizes seven major chakras identified with plexuses of the physical body, plus many other minor sites; Buddhism recognizes four such centres.

Copts | members of the early Christian church originating and centred in Egypt, employing the Alexandrian rite, and Monophysites until becoming Roman Catholic in 1741.

Cytoplasm | cellular mass surrounding a nucleus.

Dolmen | megalithic monument; large stone plate laid across other vertical stones.

Electrode | pointed instrument conducting an electric current into a nonmetallic body.

Electrolysis | chemical changes created in a substance by passing an electric current through it; the instrument is an electrolyser.

Electromagnetic wave | propagated by variations of intensity in electric and magnetic fields, they traverse free space at the speed of light; can be any of the following types of wave: gamma, infra-red, radio, ultra-violet, visible light, or X-ray.

Electron | the lightest of the subatomic elementary particles of matter, carrying a negative charge which is considered the basic constituent of electricity; eV = electron volt.

Elementals | elements or energies of the subhuman world; nature spirits.

Epicurus | Greek philosopher of the third and fourth centuries before Christ.

Etheric body | irradiative energy field surrounding the physical body; revealed by the Kirlian process.

Faraday cage | enclosure formed of a metallic grille with tight links, so as to create a shield against external electrostatic phenomena.

Gamma | gamma rays are emitted spontaneously by some radioactive substances; they are analogous to X-rays but have a shorter wavelength.

Genius locii	the genius of the site.
Geobiology	the study of the influence of the earth and the site on all forms of life: man, plant, and animal.
Geomancy	divination; an ancient Chinese science establishing the cosmo-telluric equilibrium of the habitat.
Geopathogenic	having a negative influence on health and emanating from a precise point of the site.
Geo-rhythmogram	a graph showing in kOhm the cutaneous resistance of a person. It is used to demonstrate the harmfulness of a site or of a material on a human being.
Gigahertz	a modulation of frequency equal to one billion vibrations per second.
Hara	Japanese conception of the physical centre of man; the concentration of physical force in the lower abdomen.
H network	gridwork of telluric rays covering the globe, named after Dr. E. Hartmann, the medical doctor who discovered them; two metres (6 feet 6 inches) apart from north to south and 2.5 metres (8 feet) apart from east to west.
Interference	the phenomenon of reinforcement and weakening produced by the superposition of several vibratory movements.
Ion	an electrically-charged atom derived from the electrolytic dissociation of a body, from having gained or lost electrons.
kHertz	kHz = 1000 vibrations per second.
Kirlian	Electrophotographic process named after its Russian inventor; an object is placed over a sheet of unexposed film and then receives a burst of electricity from a metal plate beneath – when developed the typi-

cal Kirlian corona appears; this process reveals the etheric or energetic body.

kOhm = 1000 ohms, an ohm being the unit for measuring electrical resistance.

Kundalini in yoga, the latent energy lying coiled in the coccyx at the base of the spine and focalizing the fire of Initiation.

Laser Light Amplification by Stimulated Emission of Radiation, utilizing the natural oscillation of atoms or molecules between energy levels.

Mandala Hindu and Buddhist ritual design composed of a circle within a square, often with another square and more circles within the outermost circle, frequently further decorated with various symbolic designs, and used as an object of meditation.

Mantra sacred word or phrase endowed with energy, vibrations and sounds leading to a subtle level of contemplation and used as an instrument of meditation.

Megahertz = one million vibrations per second.

Menhir megalithic monument; tall stone standing vertically.

Microwaves relatively short electromagnetic waves extending upward from 1000 megahertz.

Millivolt mV = one thousandth of a volt.

Naga Hindu and Tibetan symbol having the body of a serpent and signifying subterranean forces.

Naos that part of an Egyptian temple having the strongest vibration and reserved for intiates.

Newton Sir Isaac Newton (1643–1727), eminent mathematician, physicist, philosopher and alchemist famed for his formulation of the three fundamental laws of mechanics and the law of gravitation, as well as the discovery of the composition of white light.

Ohmmeter
an instrument which indicates resistance measured in ohms; used to create a geo-rhythmogram by measuring a person's cutaneous resistance.

Pentagram
figure representing a five-pointed star.

Radiesthésie
divination based on detecting radiation emitted by a body; a subjective method and parapsychological discipline; permits, among other things, determining the energetic intensity of a site.

Radionic
apparatus projecting resonance against a distant target.

Shiva
Hindu god incarnating eternal cosmic energy, the supreme creative force over endless time; one of the most complex of the Hindu gods, combining seemingly contradictory qualities such as destruction-regeneration, asceticism-sensuality, benevolence-wrath; usually depicted in dance, thus maintaining multiple natural phenomena in life and liberating numberless souls from the trap of illusion.

Stupa
Buddhist shrines and commemorative monuments of a characteristic architectural form.

Telluric
relating to an electric current which is detected near the earth's surface; influence of this current on the habitat and the inhabitant.

Yin and Yang
the two complementary principles or forces in Chinese cosmology, expressing a dualism found in all aspects of life: negative vs. positive, feminine vs. masculine, terrestrial vs. celestial, dark vs. light, absorbing vs. penetrating, Earth vs. Heaven, etc.

Bibliography

★★1) Blanche Merz, "Telluric Rays and their Influence on the Living World", CH-1803 Chardonne, Switzerland: Institut de Recherches en Géobiologie, Château de Chardonne, 1974.

★★2) Ing. Rob. Hartmann, "Wetter, Boden, Mensch" (brochure no. 13/1983), D-6930 Eberbach am Neckar.

★★3) "The Cosmogony of Urantia", Chicago 60614: Urantia Foundation, 533 Diversey Parkway, 1961.

Rémi Alexandre, "Votre Lit Est-Il à la Bonne Place: Introduction à la Géobiologie", 75009 Paris: Editions KA, 13 rue Sainte-Cécile, 1981.

J. B. Bateman, "Microwave Magic", ONRL C 14–77, London: Office of Naval Research.

Louis Charpentier, "Les Mystères de la Cathédrale de Chartres", Saffron Walden, The C. W. Daniel Co.

Ing. Robert Endroes, ed. by Prof. K. E. Lotz, "Die Strahlung der Erde und ihre Wirkung auf das Leben", D-5630 Remscheid 1: Paffrath-Verlag.

F. Frachebois, "Les Menhirs d'Acq", F–25000 Besançon: F. Frachebois, architect. (Creator of the sketches in this book.)

Tom Graves, "Needles of Stone", London W14: Turnstone Press Ltd., 1978.

Dr. Med. Ernst Hartman, "Krankheit als Standortproblem", Heidelberg: K. F. Haug-Verlag.

Koenig, Krueger, Lang, and Soenning, "Biologic Effects of Environmental Electromagnetism", New York, Heidelberg, Berlin: Springer, 1981.

Prof. Ing. Herbert Koenig, "Unsichtbare Umwelt", Munich: Heinz-Moos Verlag, 1974.

Maurice Krafft, "La Terre, Une Planète Vivante", Paris: Hachette.

Prof. K. E. Lotz, "Do You Want to Live Healthily?",

D-5630 Remscheid, 1: Paffrath-Verlag, 1982.

John Michell, "The Earth Spirit", London: Thames & Hudson, 1975.

D. Milner, "Experiment/Schoepfung", Freiburg im Breisgau: Bauer-Verlag.

Henry Moray, "Radiant Energy", Salt Lake City: Cosray Research Institute, 1960.

———, "The Sea of Energy in Which the Earth Floats", Salt Lake City: Cosray Research Institute.

Raymond Ruyer, "La Gnose de Princeton", Paris: Editions Fayard.

R. A. Schwaller de Lubicz, "Le Temple de l'homme", Dervy-Livres.

Theodore Schwenk, "Le Chaos sensible", Paris: Triades.

E. Smart, "The Loom of Creation", Saffron Walden, The C. W. Daniel Co.

Henri Vincenot, "Les Etoiles de Compostelle" (fiction), Paris: Denoel.

Richard Wilhelm, "Yi-King, Le Livre des Transformations", Paris: Librairie de Médicis.

Alfred Watkins, "The Old Straight Track", London: Garnstone Press Ltd., 1972.

Translator's Notes on Egyptian Names and Places

French	English
Abydos	Abydos
Akhenaton	*Akhenaton*, Ikhnaton
Amenophis III	Amenhotep
Ankh	Ankh
Beth	not found
Chéops	*Khufu*, Cheops
Chephren	Khafre
Denderrah	Dendera, *Dandarah*
Edfou	*Edfu*, Idfu
Ghiza, Giza	Giza
Hathor	Hathor
Imhotep	Imhotep
Ka	Ka
Kom-Ombo	Kawn Umbu
Naos	not found
Neters	not found
Nout	*Nut,* Neuth, Nuit
Philae	Philae
Ptha	Ptah
Ra	Ra
Sakkara	Saqqara
Sekmet	*Sekhmet*, Sekhet
Sobek	*Sebek*, Sebeq, Sobk
Tell-el-Amarna	Tel-el-Amarna
Ureus	not found
Zoser	Djoser

Sources: Encyclopedia Britannica; The Macmillian Encyclopedia (desk); Columbia Viking Desk Encyclopedia; The Reader's Encyclopedia (Benet); Chambers Biographical Dictionary; The Times Atlas of the World (rev. ed.); Webster's New Collegiate Dictionary.